THE PA
JOYCE AND
A Touris

CH00543733

Brian O'Shea and Sean Donlon
© 1998 / 2007 / 2012 Brian O'Shea anᵤ ᵤₑₐₙ ᵤₒₙₗₒₙ. ₐₗₗ ᵣᵢgₕₜₛ ᵣₑₛₑᵣᵥₑᵤ.

First published in 1998 by London Irish Literary Travel 62b Hereford Road
London W2 5AJ.

Artwork - Bernadette O'Shea and Mary O'Shea
Cover Design - Marysia O'Shea
Photograph of Samuel Beckett - John Minihan

Acknowledgements

Grateful thanks to:
Edward Beckett, Anne Bihan, Michael Condon, Michelle Eastwick, Linda
Fallon, Martin Halvey, Grace Holtkamp, Neville Keery, Claire McMonagle,
Maureen McNeill, Patrick Maher, Mary Marcus, John Minihan, Rhiannon
Moss, Tony Murray, Noreen Nolan, Joanne O'Brien, Mark O'Leary, Julia
O'Shea, Colin Presly, Gaël Staunton, Hilary Staunton and Nicolas Tivollier
for their contributions, suggestions, assistance, encouragement and advice.

Maureen McNeill who sadly passed away in February this year will be
greatly missed. Maureen was the person who took on the task of setting up
and working on London Irish Literary Travel's first website and also helped
to proof read the second edition of this guide. A lover of books, a librarian
and a teacher for many years in London secondary schools let us hope
Maureen is having a well deserved rest and will continue to encourage and
guide us from some heavenly *café litteraire.*

And grateful thanks to:
Yale University Press for their kind permission to include an extract from
The World of Samuel Beckett 1906 - 1946 by Lois Gordon, and a special
thanks to Michael Regan for his patience and expertise in again setting up
the text, pagination and lay out of a new edition and presenting the diverse
material supplied in such a polished format. Finally, many thanks to Dublin
Port Company for their support for London Irish Literary Travel and this
guide.

THE PARIS OF
JOYCE AND BECKETT
A Tourist Guide

Whilst the authors have taken great care in producing this guide to ensure that the information contained is correct they cannot accept any responsibility for any errors which may appear.

ISBN 978-0-9532898-2-0
Printed by: Imprint.Digital.Com, Upton Pyne, Devon EX5 5HY, UK

THE PARIS OF
JOYCE AND BECKETT
A Tourist Guide

THE PARIS OF
JOYCE AND BECKETT
A Tourist Guide

CONTENTS (Continued)   **PAGE**

INTRODUCTION

This guide to Paris consists of nine itineraries around the city in the footsteps of Joyce and Beckett. The itineraries are based on imaginary scenarios concerning Joyce and Beckett at different points in their lives from when Joyce came to Paris with his family in 1920 to 1953 when Beckett's *En Attendant Godot* was first performed.

In a city devoted to intellectual adventure, philosophical speculation and literary expression, Joyce and Beckett were very much to the fore throughout much of the twentieth century; Joyce in the twenties and thirties and Beckett from the fifties to the eighties.

This guide is not, of course, a critique of their work or of their ideas, but rather a light-hearted, although sometimes serious, wandering through the city in which they lived so much of their lives and which still remains much as it was in their day. It is hoped by the authors that it will be a useful and entertaining companion for visitors to Paris with literary interests and perhaps also helpful to students keen to discover more about these two Irish writers who had such an influence on twentieth century literature.

New features of our third edition are photos by Joanne O'Brien, some Joycean items to mark Joyce's recent 70th anniversary including an essay by Grace Holtkamp, a poem, *Seine et Liffey* and, finally, some selected passages from *Finnegans Wake*. There are also fold up maps of the various itineraries within the guide's accompanying literary travel pack as well as the reference map on the back cover which shows the various itineraries in their overall Parisian setting. Any suggestions for future editions are most welcome and it only remains to wish our readers ...*un bon sejour a Paris et bonnes balades litteraires!*

ITINERARY I: BIBLIOTHÈQUE NATIONALE - RUE DE L'ASSOMPTION - RUE DU FAUBOURG ST HONORE

SCENARIO: It is summer 1920 and Joyce, after a hard afternoon's work on *Ulysses* at the Bibliothèque Nationale (rue de Richelieu), is enjoying a leisurely journey back to his flat in rue de l'Assomption (XVIieme) via Pantheon and the Bibliothèque St Genevieve where he hopes to check some classical references. Later in the evening he is due to dine with Wyndham Lewis and T.S Eliot in a restaurant on rue du Faubourg St Honore.

SUMMARY: Start of Itinerary:
Main entrance of Bibliothèque Nationale, Rue de Richelieu - Metro Quatre Septembre

10 - 12 min. walk to: Church of St-Eustache

No.47 bus to: Hotel de Ville

6 - 7 min. walk to: Notre Dame

17 - 18 min. walk to: Pantheon - Bibliothèque St

(or 10 min No.47 bus ride)   Genevieve

9 - 10 min. walk to: Ecole Normale Supérieure

20 min. coffee break: Rue des Feuillantines / Rue Gay Lussac

7 - 10 min. bus ride (No.38) to: Denfert Rochereau

20 min. Metro journey to: Passy (Metro)

7 - 8 min. walk to: Maison de Balzac (Rue Raynouard)

5 min. walk to: Rue de l'Assomption

20 min. coffee break: Place du Docteur Hayem

5 min. walk to: Ranelagh (Metro)

15 min. Metro journey to: Miromesnil (Metro)

2 - 3 min. walk to: Rue du Faubourg St Honore

20 min. Metro journey from: Miromesnil to Les Halles (Metro) - change Strasbourg - St Denis

3 min. walk to: Quigley's Point (Irish Pub) 5 Rue du Jour

DURATION: About 3 hours.

ITINERARY

The main entrance of the Bibliothèque Nationale (National Library) is at No. 58 in the rue de Richelieu - the nearest Metro station being Quatre Septembre. The Bibliothèque Nationale is where Joyce used to spend his days studying during his first visit to Paris from 1902 - 1903. At one time the residence of Cardinal Mazarin, it holds copies of every book published in France since 1537. To start our journey it is a short walk along rue de la Vrillière, past the Banque de France, across rue Croix des Petits Champs, and along rue Coquilliere to the Church of St Eustache. Eustache was a Christian Martyr and the church was modelled on Notre Dame when it was built in the 16th century. St Eustache is particularly noted for its religious concerts and especially its Gregorian Midnight Mass at Christmas.

From St Eustache it is approximately a 20 minute walk along rue Rambuteau towards Rambuteau Metro then turning right down rue Beaubourg and rue du Renard to reach the Hotel de Ville (City Hall), or alternatively you can take the No. 47 bus from rue du Grenier St Lazare at the far side of Bd de Sebastopol. One can imagine Joyce pausing here to reflect that 50 years earlier, on 4th September 1870, the Hotel de Ville was the scene of the proclamation of the Third Republic - an event that was to lead to the Prussian siege of Paris and later the Paris Commune. During the winter of 1870-71 Parisians were reduced to not only eating domestic pets and rats but also the Zoo animals. The suppression of the Paris Commune by 70,000 troops loyal to the French Government, which had accepted the peace treaty with Prussia, included a week of desperate fighting from street to street in Paris in May 1871 which claimed far more victims than the Revolution of 1789. The Communards made a last stand in Père- Lachaise cemetery and those captured alive were shot at dawn the next morning. The events in Dublin in 1916 - the Easter Rising - would still no doubt have been very much on Joyce's mind in 1920,

4

although he never became actively involved in politics.
From the Hotel de Ville, and crossing the Seine at Pont d'Arco, it
is only a short walk to the Cathedral of Notre Dame. This is where
Joyce often attended vespers during his stay in Paris in 1902 -
1903, reflecting his life long love of music. To reach the Pantheon
and the Bibliothèque Ste Genevieve on foot from Notre Dame, it
is a brisk 15 minute walk down rue St.
Jacques turning left at Place Edmond
Rostand, and up into rue Soufflott.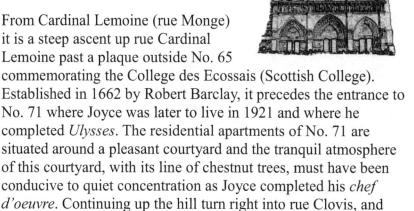
Alternatively, it is possible to catch a
No.47 bus from the Cite Parvis - Notre
Dame to Cardinal Lemoine (Metro).

From Cardinal Lemoine (rue Monge)
it is a steep ascent up rue Cardinal
Lemoine past a plaque outside No. 65
commemorating the College des Ecossais (Scottish College).
Established in 1662 by Robert Barclay, it precedes the entrance to
No. 71 where Joyce was later to live in 1921 and where he
completed *Ulysses*. The residential apartments of No. 71 are
situated around a pleasant courtyard and the tranquil atmosphere
of this courtyard, with its line of chestnut trees, must have been
conducive to quiet concentration as Joyce completed his *chef
d'oeuvre*. Continuing up the hill turn right into rue Clovis, and
passing the Church of St. Etienne du Mont on the left you emerge
into the Place Ste Genevieve and then the Place du Pantheon. A
truly stunning vista can be seen, dominated by the Eiffel Tower
some four kilometres away.

The Montagne Ste Genevieve, the patroness of Paris, on which the
enormous bulk of the Pantheon rests, was the place to which in the
early Middle Ages teachers and students of theology, wishing to
escape the greater orthodoxy and stricter atmosphere of the Ile de
la Cite and the schools of Notre Dame, came to settle, thus
beginning the expansion of Paris onto the Left Bank. The

Pantheon, now a spectacular monument, was originally meant to be a church erected by a grateful Louis XV for recovery from an illness in 1744, but was deconsecrated by the Constituent Assembly in 1791 then re-consecrated under Napoleon, relaicised by Louis Phillippe, and finally confirmed in this status in 1885 when it received the ashes of Victor Hugo.

The Bibliothèque Ste. Genevieve - No. 10 Place du Pantheon - built close to the site of the former abbey of Ste Genevieve, was often used by Joyce particularly during his first visit to the city in 1902-03 when he used to study there nightly before returning to his lodgings in Hotel Corneille, rue Corneille. A 10 minute walk down rue d'Ulm past Notre Dame du Liban (Our Lady of Lebanon) - the rue des Irlandais lies just opposite - and past Institut Curie, brings you to the Ecole Normale Supérieure. This was where Beckett was later to study in 1928 at the same time as Jean Paul Sartre and Simone Weil. In Joyce's first stay in Paris he had briefly attended the Faculty of Science in the Sorbonne, hoping to become a doctor, however, in the spring of 1903 his mother's terminal illness obliged him to return to Dublin. She died in August of that year aged only 44. Joyce was 21. Outside the Ecole Normale Supérieure you will find an engraved notice proclaiming its establishment by the Convention on 9th Brumaire, year (Revolutionary Calendar) 3 (1792) and by a further decree of the First Empire dated 17th March 1808.

This is probably a good time to stop for a coffee. There are cafes nearby in the rue des Feuillantines and rue Gay Lussac, some of them almost certainly frequented by Beckett in his day and also perhaps by Joyce some years earlier.

From the corner of rue des Feuillantines and rue Gay Lussac it is a 5 minute walk to the No.38 bus stop Boulevard St Michel / rue Auguste Comte. Walking up rue Gay Lussac turn left into rue des Ursulines, right into rue St Jacques, and left again into rue de l'Abbe. It is then a short bus ride down the lower end of the Bd. St Michel, past the hospital of St Vincent de Paul, to Place Denfert Rochereau.

From Denfert Rochereau Metro it is a 20 minute train journey to Passy where Joyce would have alighted to return to rue de l'Assomption. Taking Ligne 6 (Direction-Etoile) the line emerges onto an elevated section before Sevres Lecourbe and is somewhat reminiscent of the "L" railway in New York. At Bir Hakeim the line crosses the Seine with incredible views in both directions. Immediately to the right lies the Eiffel Tower and also to the right Sacre Coeur can be discerned on the horizon. To the left long lines of barges can be seen moored along Port de Grenelle, and by the Pont de Grenelle you will see a replica of the original Statue of Liberty in New York, given to France by the Parisian community in the U.S in 1885 (and erected in 1889).

From Passy (Metro) the Maison de Balzac is a 7-8 min. walk along rue des Eaux, rue Charles Dickens, Avenue Marcel Proust and into rue Raynouard. It was here that Balzac wrote most of *La Comedie Humaine* between 1840 and 1847. Neither Joyce nor Beckett shared Balzac's or Dickens's approach to the novel, or their enthusiasm for it in its conventional form, but this would be straying into controversial territory! From Maison de Balzac it is a 5-6 min. walk to the lower end of rue de l'Assomption where the Joyce family first had a flat in Paris. The Convent of the Assumption founded by Ste Marie Eugenie de Jesus lies further up the street on the left.

Another break for refreshments might be in order and at the lower end of rue de l'Assomption lies the Place Docteur Hayem, a pleasant crossroads where five streets meet and a variety of cafes can be found. Ranelagh Metro can then be reached by walking again up rue de l'Assomption and turning right at the intersection with Avenue Mozart. The nearby Jardins de Ranelagh were one of

sites for Montgolfier type ascents, notably by Pilatre de Rozier.
They are named after Lord Ranelagh as a café-dance hall similar
to one created by Lord Ranelagh in Chelsea existed on the green
in the 1770s following permission given to a man called Morison
by the Governor de la Muette. Marie Antoinette was said to have
danced there. The journey to Miromesnil takes about 20 minutes
at most and the rue du Faubourg St Honore is close to the Metro.
Joyce was fond of dining in this very expensive area of Paris, and
as well as the rue du Faubourg St Honore he often dined in
restaurants in the nearby Champs Elysees. A particular favourite
was Fouquets where his tips were remembered for many years
afterwards.

Finally, returning to Miromesnil Metro it is a 20 min. journey to
Les Halles, (changing at Strasbourg St Denis), which takes us
back to almost where the itinerary began. Walking up rue
Montmartre and past the church of St Eustache you've probably
earned a visit to Quigley's Point - an Irish Pub that can be found
around the corner at no.5 rue du Jour.

ITINERARY II: PLACE DUPLEIX - ALLEE DES CYGNES -
CHATELET

SCENARIO: This scene is set in the early spring of 1924 and Joyce has promised Ford Madox Ford an extract from *Work in Progress* for his 'Transatlantic Review'. Behind schedule with proof reading he nevertheless decides to have a brief rest and go on a mini-odyssey to the Ile Des Cygnes for a refreshing walk by the river. Leaving his temporary residence in a hotel, rue Blaise Desgoffe, Joyce journeys by Metro from St Placide, changing at Montparnasse, to Dupleix. It is a raw fresh February day and after alighting Joyce feels a chill gust from the river, in the words of a contemporary poet he had been 'warm and snug sitting in the Metro'. Turning up his collar he goes down the stairs from the elevated platform and makes a brief detour to Place Dupleix - where in the everyday atmosphere of this quiet unpretentious fifteenth arrondisement square his thoughts are on his epic new work which he will be engaged on for another fourteen years.

Walking around Place Dupleix Joyce observes a concierge carrying a bag of French loaves back from a nearby boulangerie and thinks of James Stephen's celebrated novel, *The Charwoman's Daughter* (1912), a story of life in the Dublin slums. Stephens was to become one of Joyce's closest friends - they even shared the same birthday on February 2nd 1882 - and in later years Joyce seriously considered asking Stephens to complete *Finnegans Wake* due to his failing eyesight.

As he walks, Joyce is thinking of endings and
new beginnings, death and resurrection,
absorption and separation, time and tide, ebb
and flow. Crossing the first half of Pont de Bir
Hakeim, (Pont de Passy in 1924), he descends
the steps and proceeds to walk along the entire
length of the Allee des Cygnes towards the tip
of the island. On his way he observes some
bargemen at work on a passing coal laden
vessel and then some municipal employees
painting riverside benches. He has a sudden
but fleeting longing for *la vie quotidienne de
travail, la vie ordinaire* of routine, stability,
predictability, communal endeavour and
belonging, but he has chosen his path and
continues his walk with some sadness as, in an
illuminated moment, he sees and feels deeply
the sheer fragility of everyday happiness.

As he walks along the quiet tree lined path
down the centre of the island he reflects on his
artistic mission to make the quotidian, the
transient world of everyday life, a thing of
permanence and beauty. Watching the
bargemen at work he recalls his story in
Dubliners, A Little Cloud where one of the
main characters, Ignatius Gallagher, extols the
joys of Paris to his downtrodden friend, Little
Chandler, who has a steady but unglamorous
job and family responsibilities. It's not all fine
living and gaiety he thinks to himself, and
recalls with a chuckle Ignatius Gallaghers
excoriation of printers and proofs! Finally

Joyce reaches the tip of the island where the branches of the Seine rejoin to almost form a bay and he reflects for a while on the Liffey, which in his new work he will personify as Anna Livia Plurabelle, and other phenomena of the natural world.

With some satisfaction he recalls the opening lines of his new *Work in Progress* which in time will become *Finnegans Wake* and, his mood lifting, he begins to make his way back to the bridge and the opposite bank. Just as he is about to ascend the steps to the Pont de Grenelle he encounters a party of young Italian sailors coming down to visit the Statue of Liberty at the tip of the island. Nodding quietly to himself he mutters 'here comes everybody', and after exchanging a friendly greeting with the boisterous marine tourists he crosses the bridge, has a coffee in the Avenue de Versailles, and catches the bus back to Châtelet for the Metro connection to St Placide.

SUMMARY:	Start of Itinerary: Dupleix (Metro) Ligne 6
3 min. walk to:	Place Dupleix
6 - 7 min. walk around:	Place Dupleix
3 min. walk to:	Rue George Bernard Shaw
9 - 10 min. walk to:	Pont de Bir Hakeim

10 - 12 min. walk down:	Allee des Cygnes
5 min. stop:	Statue de la Liberte
5 min. walk to:	Avenue de Versailles (Place Clement Ader)
	(15 - 20 min. coffee break)
No.72 bus (15-20 min) to:	Châtelet
DURATION:	About 1¼- 1½ hours.

ITINERARY

In his contribution, the *"Mind of Joyce"* to *The Irish Mind -
Exploring Intellectual Traditions*, Mark Patrick Hederman
describes Joyce as 'an unusually isolated explorer'. In 1924 his
novel *Ulysses*, condemned by one critic as "literary bolshevism",
had achieved a ground breaking departure from previous literary
norms and conventions, not only in its stream of consciousness
technique but also in its realistic, yet highly imaginative, and
almost *cinema verite* like, portrayal of modern life. Jeri Johnson in
her introduction to the OUP edition of *Ulysses* invites us to watch
the technique of the *monologue interieure,* the inner verbalisation
of consciousness in action, how, within a few words, Joyce is able
to convey intimacy, immediacy and ineradicable distinctions of
character. Over the next 14 years *Ulysses* was to be followed by
the even more convention defying, densely packed with meaning,
Finnegans Wake.

However, in the early spring of 1924, Joyce had every reason to
rest on his laurels. After just three and a half years in Paris he had
carved a secure niche for himself in 'the last of the human cities'.
He had acquired many new friends and as the author of *Ulysses*
was enjoying widespread critical acclaim, public controversy and
financial security. His family was almost grown up and a long
period of relative stability and contentment in Square de Robiac
was not far off. But, first reactions to his *Work in Progress*, even
from friends and supporters, were to say the least disappointing.
No-one knew quite what to make of what Hederman describes as
'not a novel, not a play, not a poem - neither poetry nor prose but
a work of art'. Harriet Shaw Weaver, Joyce's most faithful and
certainly most generous supporter, confessed to being puzzled by
Work in Progress and intimated that Joyce was wasting his talent.
He was deeply affected by her criticisms and those of others,
including his brother Stanislaus, and for a time his usual self
assurance deserted him. As often in his life, a long walk soon

13

helped to restore equilibrium.

Place Dupleix is a quiet unpretentious square in the 15th. It can be reached by turning right when coming out of Dupleix Metro and then by turning left down rue Auguste Bartoldi. Its main feature is the church of St. Leon which has a distinctive gherkin shaped spire and which is also built with cheerful cream coloured bricks. Leaving the square walk up rue Daniel Stern. A two to three minute walk up this street will lead you to the street now known as rue George Bernard Shaw. On the street sign the epithet says simply 'Ecrivain Irlandais 1856 - 1950'. (NB in 1924 this area was a cavalry barracks). Born 26 years before Joyce, Shaw was to outlive him by 9 years. Shaw himself was, of course, another great Dublin writer, and O'Casey, Beckett, and Joyce would all have read and been influenced by his plays with their lengthy prefaces, full of Shavian wit and paradox. Joyce did indeed refer approvingly to Shaw's own lack of conventionality saying that 'he [Shaw] seldom thought or behaved as convention demands'.

In 1924, with the production for the first time on 26th March of *St Joan* at the New Theatre, Shaw was at the height of his fame and powers. He had campaigned vigorously against the unnecessary and terrible slaughter of the First World War - as early as 1914 he had written *Common Sense About The War* - and despite being anti-war was more secure in the affections of the public than ever. He was soon to receive the Nobel Prize in 1925. Joyce and Shaw shared an admiration for Ibsen, Joyce even going to the extent of learning Norwegian so that he could read Ibsen's work in its original language. However, although Joyce was complimentary of Shaw's work, Shaw had been less than complimentary about *Ulysses* - although presumably he would have enjoyed *Dubliners* and the *Portrait of The Artist as a Young Man*.

Continuing up rue Daniel Stern and rue Clodion, a right turn into Bd. De Grenelle leads you to Bir Hakeim Metro. Just before Bir

Hakeim Metro, and while crossing the side road, rue Saint Saens, there is a tremendous first sight of the Eiffel Tower. Despite its relatively light weight - 7000 tons - the tower we are assured never sways more than 4½ inches (12cm) but its height can vary, depending on the temperature, by as much as 6 inches (15cm). At the top of Bd. De Grenelle cross over to the left, and then over the Quai de Grenelle before crossing Pont de Bir Hakeim, and at the half way point descend down the steps to the Ile Des Cygnes. Near the bridge there is a monument to wartime deportees who were assembled nearby before their tragic journey.

The Ile Des Cygnes (Isle of Swans) is a narrow island, reinforced by concrete embankments, of over 1km in length in the middle of the Seine. Lined with trees on either side the Allee des Cygnes leads down the entire length of the island. After about a 10 minute walk the head and shoulders of the Statue de la Liberte looms suddenly into view in an almost disconcerting fashion. This mini version of the New York statue is nevertheless quite imposing in its mid-river setting and on one side of the statue is written the legend

'Cette statue a été offerte a la ville de Paris par la communuaté parisienne des Etats-Unis d'Amerique'

(This statue was presented to the city of Paris by the Parisian community in the U.S)

Erected in 1889 the statue was restored in 1986.

To reach the statue one has to go down the steps on the left of the Allee des Cygnes and walk under the bridge. The surface beneath the bridge is made up of gravel and may be a little rough underfoot. One wonders if a smoother approach to the statue would enhance Franco-American relations! N.B. the statue is in quite an isolated spot and is best visited in daytime.

Returning to Joyce he would no doubt have looked out on the quite dramatically wide Seine at this point and seen the lines of barges and even perhaps some small ships. Would he, like Beckett later - and with whom he often completed this walk - have dwelt on the joyous conflowing on of the river's two arms? Very likely, Joyce and Beckett both had a love of the outdoors, Joyce once remarking to Eugene Jolas, proprietor, with his wife Maria, of *transition*, 'an international quarterly for creative expression', that mountains and rivers "are the phenomena that will remain when all the people and their governments will have vanished". Beckett was also an especially acute observer of nature e.g. noting in one memorable passage in *Molloy* how 'in the evening light the hills that some call mountains turn indigo' and how subtly different colour tones can hint at the existence of hidden valleys in ways which find no verbal expression, but are none the less perceptible to the senses.

Perhaps the opening words of *Work In Progress* 'riverrun, past Eve and Adams, from swerve of shore to bend of bay' would be running through Joyce's mind. Observing the busy scene of barges along the quais and on the river he may also have thought of the theories of Giambattista Vico (1688 - 1744), one of his favourite philosophers along with Dante and Bruno, concerning the circular nature of history and successive ages or epochs recurring in turn indefinitely. In the same way that the last words of *Finnegans Wake* lead on again to its opening words without any break in the sense, so that the tale of here comes everybody / Humphrey Chimpden Earwicker / Everyman and Anna Livia Plurabelle starts all over again… and again.

But now it is time for a coffee break, and going up the steps to the busy Pont de Grenelle and taking a short traverse along rue

Maurice Bourdet (Journaliste-Resistant) you will find a selection of cafes in the Avenue de Versailles. Ondes (Waves), opposite Maison de Radio France, could be your choice. One can imagine Joyce sipping his coffee in Avenue de Versailles and thinking back to 1920 when he and his family lived in much less luxurious surroundings in the nearby rue de l'Assomption, almost literally around the corner. The bus stop for the No.72 back to Châtelet and the city centre lies about 100 metres down Avenue de Versailles on the other side of the road. In normal traffic it should take no more than 25 minutes and much less at weekends. The No.72 passes along Ave du President Kennedy, Avenue du New York, Cours de la Reine, Quai des Tuileries, Quai du Louvre - with stunning river views along the way - before reaching Quai de la Megisserie and Pl. du Châtelet. Sandwiched between Theatre Musical de Paris and Theatre de la Ville, the bustling Place du Chatelet seems an appropriate location to end the itinerary after the quiet Allee des Cygnes and Statue de la Liberte.

An interesting alternative ending would be to alight at Concorde and travel from Concorde Metro (six stops, 8-9 minutes) to Porte Maillot Metro, (direction La Defense), where the James Joyce pub is situated close by at no.71 Boulevard Gouvion St Cyr. This is a lively bar that caters for all age groups. Exit no. 2 is the correct exit from the Metro and if, when you emerge - you need to follow the signs for 'sortie 2' for a good 5 minutes up and down stairs – if you see a restaurant called Chez Clement you have got it right first time as this is no. 99 Bd Gouvion St Cyr and the James Joyce Pub is at no.71.

ITINERARY III: MONTPARNASSE - JARDIN JAMES JOYCE - GARE DE LYON - BOULEVARD ST GERMAIN

SCENARIO: It is 1928 and a chilly morning in late autumn. The young Samuel Beckett and some acquaintances from the Ecole Normale Supérieure, where he has recently begun to lecture, are coming to the end of a night of animated discussion at a café in Montparnasse.

Suddenly Beckett remembers that he has promised Joyce that he would meet a friend of his arriving that day from Italy at the Gare de Lyon and take him to Sylvia Beach's bookshop, rue de l'Odeon.

He returns briefly to his hotel and takes the Metro towards Gare de Lyon. As it is still early in the morning he decides to alight en route at Quai de la Gare for a coffee in the warmth of one of the cafes in the busy area around the Goods Station. Then keeping his appointment at the Gare de Lyon he goes later to the Ecole Normale Superieure. In the afternoon he has an early finish and strolls through the Jardin du Luxembourg towards another café in Boulevard St Germain where he finds himself in the company of Hemingway and Joyce.

SUMMARY: Start of Itinerary:
Le Select, 99 Bd. Montparnasse - Metro Vavin.

5 min. walk to: Edgar Quinet (Metro)

15 - 16 min. Metro journey to:	Quai de la Gare
4 - 5 min walk to:	Jardin James Joyce
6 - 7 min walk to:	Café de la Bibliotheque (Avenue de France)
10 min. walk or No.89 bus to:	Quai de la Gare
2 - 3 min. Metro journey to:	Bercy: Direction Nation (Ligne 6)
8 - 9 min. walk to:	Gare de Lyon (SNCF)
10 min. bus ride (No.63) to:	Odeon
2 min. walk to:	Rue de l'Odeon
	(20 min coffee break)
Long walk to:	Ecole Normale Supérieure
10 min. walk to:	Jardin du Luxembourg
Long walk to:	Café de Flore, Bd. St Germain
DURATION:	About 3 Hours.

ITINERARY

Starting from Vavin Metro (Ligne 4) it is only a two minute walk
to Le Select. Le Select was one of a group of cafes in Boulevard
Montparnasse much frequented by writers and artists in the
Twenties and Thirties. The Americans Ernest Hemingway and
Scott Fitzgerald, visiting English writers such as T.S Eliot and
Ezra Pound, Anais Nin and George Orwell as well as Joyce and
Beckett themselves were some of the many expatriates who, in
Hemingway's memorable phrase,
were part of 'the moveable feast'
that was the Paris of the period.
Le Select, Le Dome, La Coupole,
La Rotonde, and La Closerie des
Lilas further down Bd.
Montparnasse were an important
part of Parisian intellectual,
literary and artistic life. Les

La Rotunde

Trianons, Joyce's favourite restaurant, was located at the station
end of the Boulevard Place de Rennes but is no longer there - the
site now known as Place du 18 Juin 1940.

From Le Select it is only a short walk down R. Delambre, also
much frequented by Joyce and Beckett, to the Metro at Edgar
Quinet. From Edgar Quinet the best way to get to Gare de Lyon is
probably to take Ligne 6 to Bercy, some 10 stops, rather than
continuing to Nation, changing, and then doubling back. On the
way, and passing through St. Jacques, Beckett would have little
suspected that 33 years later he would be living in a new
apartment block, Boulevard St Jacques, having just finished
another play - *Happy Days* - and be a dramatist of international
renown, not to mention having survived another world war and
working for the resistance in Paris and Roussillon. In 1928,
however, Beckett was still very young and not at all sure of the
path ahead.

Quai de la Gare en route to Bercy is one of many elevated stations in the Paris Metro. Earlier in the twentieth century it was the access point to the busy goods station of the Chemins de Fer d'Orleans. In recent years the whole area has been massively redeveloped centred around the huge Bibliotheque Nationale de France- Francois Mitterand.

If your thoughts are coffee centred, the Cafe de la Bibliotheque or the Frog and British Library both in Avenue de France are a bit of a trek from the metro but worth a detour. On the way, walking along the Quai de la Gare from the Metro the first turning on the right, rue George Balanchine (Choreographe), leads to Jardin James Joyce although on one side of the garden a street sign still says Square James Joyce.

It is surprising to find a Square dedicated to Joyce in the 13th arrondissement given his much greater associations with the 5th, 6th, 7th and 14th arrondissements. Would Joyce have felt entirely comfortable with the number 13? Nevertheless the Square is here in the 13th. Perhaps a Circle James Joyce would have been more appropriate?

However, the Jardin/Square itself is very pleasant and consists almost entirely of a garden of hedge lined paths. Due to a tragic fire in the nearby Boulevard Vincent Auriol in 2005 it has been transformed by local residents into a memorial garden to the fourteen children and three adults who perished. Local residents associations wished to remember them with a garden which symbolised life and rebirth. By one of its entrances there is a brief history of the writer:

Jardin James Joyce1998
Auteur irlandais, James Joyce (1882 - 1941 est connu pour ses
nouvelles, Les Gens de Dublin (Dubliners) ses romans Dedalus
(1916), Ulysse (1922) et Finnegans Wake (1939).

In one corner of the *espace vert* (green space) which includes the garden is a stark, red brick rectangular building, Notre Dame de la Sagesse (Our Lady of Wisdom). This was the last church to be built in France in the twentieth century and one of the notable features inside is the main aisle made from Pyrenean marble which contrasts with the functional exterior.

Returning to Joyce, perhaps the Square was named after him because of the proximity of rue Valery Larbaud, the main advocate of Joyce's genius in 1920's Paris. From Square /Jardin James Joyce it is perhaps a seven or eight minute walk to the Cafe de la Bibliotheque in Avenue de France. After a coffee stop it is possible to take a number 89 straight back to Quai de la Gare. At this point the more intrepid literary tourist may wish to cross the Pont de Bercy on foot rather than take the Metro for just one stop. The bridge dates back to 1832 but was raised and strengthened in 1904. After crossing the bridge the truly monstrous Ministry of Finance building looms to one side. On the other side of the Bd de Bercy lies the equally gigantesque Palais Omnisports Paris Bercy with almost Mayan pyramid size steps leading up to its many entrances. Nearby also lies the Port de Bercy which is still operational. However, the easy way to cross the river is to take the train and it is then only a 2 minute journey to Bercy Metro.

From Bercy Metro it is a straight walk across the Place du Bataillon du Pacifique and down the rue de Bercy for about 8-9 minutes to the forecourt of the Gare de Lyon. It was here on July 8th / 9th 1920 that Joyce and his family disembarked from the train after the long journey from Trieste. Only three weeks earlier Joyce had written to his aunt saying he was returning to England, and then Ireland, but would be stopping off in Paris en route for about a week. In the event he was to stay in Paris for the next 20 years. His fortunes, then at a remarkably low ebb, were about to rise significantly. Ezra Pound had already prepared the way for Joyce in Paris literary circles as well as attending to the practical

detail of finding him a flat in Passy (rue de l'Assomption). The
first sight to have greeted Joyce, Nora, Giorgio and Lucia amidst
all the hubbub of a busy terminus would probably have been Le
Train Bleu, the main restaurant in Gare de Lyon and still there
today. Below the stairs leading to the restaurant is L'Express Bleu,
a good a place as any to have a *café allonge* or you could if you
wish ascend to Le Train Bleu and tuck in to the Sarah Bernhardt
menu which starts at 70 euro!

To return to our itinerary and to reach the Odeon from Gare de
Lyon it is probably easiest to take a No. 63 bus. This departs from
a side street, rue de Bercy, and not as one would expect from the
main Boulevard Diderot. Rue de Bercy is left and left again
coming out of the station's main entrance and the stop is about
100 metres down on the left opposite Tour de Lyon. It is then only
a short bus journey, ten minutes or so, over the Pont d'Austerlitz
to the Left Bank, Boulevard St Germain, and on to Odeon.

In 1928 Sylvia Beach's
bookshop, Shakespeare &
Company, was at No. 12 rue de
l'Odeon. The present day
Shakespeare & Company,
arguably the continent's most
famous bookshop, is situated
just opposite Notre Dame at 37
rue de la Bucherie, just behind
the Quai de Montebello. No. 12

rue de l'Odeon is now a clothes shop and a simple plaque over the
door proclaims the publication of *Ulysses* there in 1922. It is
literally only a two minute walk from the Odeon Metro across the
Carrefour de l'Odeon and straight down rue de l'Odeon where No.
12 can be found on the right.

It is difficult to overestimate the importance of Sylvia Beach to

Joyce and a large number of other expatriate writers in the Paris of
the Twenties and Thirties. Her bookshop in rue de l'Odeon,
together with that of her friend Adrienne Monnier just across the
street, was the hub of a mini-universe of literature and art, a
meeting place of some of the foremost talents of the time. It
resembled a kind of *quartier general* where expatriate writers
could pick up mail, catch up on the latest gossip, or just drop in
for a chat and a coffee with the ever sympathetic and resourceful
Sylvia. Crucially she introduced Joyce to Valery Larbaud, an
established writer, translator, and literary critic of the time. In
December 1921 he [Larbaud] gave a public lecture on *Ulysses* at
Adrienne Monnier's bookshop at No. 7 rue de l'Odeon, and his
enthusiasm for *Ulysses* was instrumental in encouraging a wave of
advance subscriptions to Shakespeare & Company for Joyce's
highly controversial novel.

Now is perhaps a good time for a coffee break and there are
several cafes in the Boulevard St Germain vicinity as well as a
good bookshop, Gibert Jeune, nearby in R. Dupuytren. Dupuytren
was the chief surgeon in the 1830s in Paris's oldest hospital, the
Hotel Dieu.

The Ecole Normale Supérieure is then a 20 minute walk across
Place de l'Odeon where Revolutionary figures such as Danton and
Camille Desmoulins used to live, around the Theatre Nationale de
l'Odeon via rue Corneille where Joyce stayed during his first visit
to Paris, down rue de Medicis, across Place Edmond Rostand, and
down the entire length of rue Gay Lussac.

Beckett was *lecteur d'anglais* at the ENS from October 1928 to
the summer of 1930 when he returned to Dublin to assume a new
post as Lecturer in French at Trinity. Whilst at ENS he also
worked on two projects, a study of Descartes for which he had
been given a £50 grant by Trinity (in those days £50 was a
substantial sum, equal to about four months wages for an ordinary

worker), and another project on the unanimiste poets Jules
Romains and Pierre Jean Jouve. Also studying at ENS at that time
were Jean Paul Sartre and Simone Weil who was later to write the
profound and popular *Waiting for God* in the Forties, and it is
interesting to speculate whether Beckett had read or heard of
Weil's *Attente de Dieu*. Beckett's own first published work, a short
story entitled *Assumption*, also appeared in this period being
published in the June 1929 edition of *transition*. Later in the same
magazine he was to write, controversially, in Joyce's defence, of
the author's right to be opaque.

The walk back from ENS to Boulevard St Germain and the Café
de Flore involves a pleasant stroll through the Jardin du
Luxembourg. Take the rue des Feuillantines up to rue Pierre
Nicole and turn left down this street. Then turn right into rue du
Val de Grace, across into l'Observatoire, Jardin Marco Polo, and
straight up through the gardens past Palais du Luxembourg (see
itinerary 4) and into rue Tournon. The rue de Tournon leads
directly into Bd. St Germain. Turning left into the boulevard the
Café de Flore, one of Paris's best known cafes litteraires, lies on
the right hand side near the Metro of St Germain des Pres. St
Germain des Pres (or St Germain of the Meadows) is named after
St Germain, a bishop of Paris who died in 576. The distance from
the Observatoire to the Café de Flore is a 20-25 minute walk.
l'Observatoire contains the Bureau International de l'Heure
(International Time Office) which has a famous speaking clock.
Consider the quiet excitement of the young Beckett finding
himself in the company of such maestros of the written word as
Joyce and Hemingway, and imagine him listening with fascination
to their conversation as he sipped a well earned demi. Paris must
have seemed like a dream come true for the young Dubliner.

Café de Flore   © Joanne O'Brien

ITINERARY IV: OPERA - MONTPARNASSE - SQUARE DE
ROBIAC

SCENARIO: Imagine it is 1930 and James Joyce is returning
home to his apartment in Square de Robiac
(7th arr.) after attending a matinee at the Paris
opera in which his friend and protégé John
O'Sullivan, the opera's leading tenor, has been
singing. O'Sullivan accompanies Joyce as far
as Le Dome, Boulevard Montparnasse, where
they have arranged to meet Beckett. On the
way there is some business to transact in
Sylvia Beach's bookshop, Shakespeare &
Company, rue de l'Odeon, and before that a
pre-lunch aperitif in a bar in rue Daunou close
to the opera.

Later Joyce continues back to Square de
Robiac stopping briefly at Editions Gallimard
just off rue du Bac, and also at the Mairie of
the 7th. Arrondissement rue de Grenelle, to
make an inquiry.

SUMMARY: Start of Itinerary:
Corner of rue Gluck and rue
Halevy (Opera Metro)

3 min. walk to: Rue Daunou

7 min. walk to: Pyramides Metro

8 min. journey to: Châtelet Metro

As it is a fine day Joyce and O'Sullivan decide to walk from Châtelet over the bridge of the Ile de la Cite to rue de l'Odeon.

20 - 25 min. walk to:	Rue Dupuytren
4 min. walk to:	12 rue de l'Odeon
20 - 25 min. walk to:	Le Dome via Jardin du Luxembourg
30 min. stop at:	Le Dome or other nearby cafes, Le Select, La Rotonde, La Coupole
7 min. walk to:	Notre Dame des Champs Metro
8 min. journey to:	Rue de Bac Metro
4 min. walk to:	Editions Gallimard, rue Montalembert
8 min. walk to:	Hotel Lenox, rue de l'Universite and back to rue du Bac Metro
10 min. walk to:	Mairie of the 7th. Arr.
20 - 25 min. walk to: (or No.69 bus ride)	Square de Robiac via Place des Invalides
7 min. walk to: (or Latour Maubourg Metro)	Ecole Militaire Metro
DURATION:	About 2¾ - 3¼ Hours.

ITINERARY

Commencing at the corner of rue Gluck and rue Halevy (Metro -
Opera) proceed across Place de l'Opera. Outside the main
entrance to the Opera are statues of Bach, Pericolini, Haydn and
Cimarosa, all dressed in classical garb. Inside, in the main foyer,
are four more statues of Rameau, Lulli, Gluck and Handel but in
more contemporary dress. Bearing right down rue de la Paix and
then left into rue Daunou Harry's New York Bar is towards the
Avenue de l'Opera end of the street on the right. Joyce, Jack
Dempsey and Hemingway used to drink here on a regular basis
and apparently Joyce's favourite drink was a dry Martini. Harry's
Bar is still run by the same Scottish family to this day. Continuing
down Avenue de l'Opera catch the
Metro at Pyramides taking Ligne 7
three stops to Châtelet.

Alighting at Châtelet, cross the Seine
at Pont Au Change perhaps making a
detour to admire the architectural
splendours of Notre Dame to the left,
and then cross again from Ile de la
Cite to the Left Bank via Pont St.
Michel. A short walk down rue
Danton then leads you to rue
Dupuytren on the far side of
Boulevard St. Germain.

Stop for a while if you wish at the interesting bookshop at No. 7
which sells both new books and *livres d'occasion* (Gibert Jeune),
and pause briefly at no. 8 rue Dupuytren which was opened in
November 1919 as the location for Shakespeare & Company, and
which is now a parfumerie. Then, turning right into rue Monsieur
Le Prince turn sharp left into rue de l'Odeon and at No. 12, (the
original site of Sylvia Beach's bookshop, Shakespeare &

Company), you will find a plaque commemorating the publication
of *Ulysses* on Joyce's birthday on 2nd February 1922.

The plaque states simply:

'*En 1922 dans cette maison Mlle Sylvia Beach publia Ulysses de
James Joyce*'

(In 1922 in this house Miss Sylvia Beach published *Ulysses* by
James Joyce)

Skirting the Theatre Nationale de l'Odeon proceed down rue
Corneille where Joyce stayed at the Hotel Corneille (no longer
there) during his first visit to Paris from December 1902 to April
1903. He was hoping to study medicine and had enrolled at the
Science Faculty of the Sorbonne, surviving by teaching English in
his spare time.

Turning right into Place Paul Claudel and into the Jardin du
Luxembourg note the Palais du Luxembourg which was built for
Maria de Medici in 1615, and which is now the home of the
French Senate. Further along to the right lies Le Petit Luxembourg
- the one time residence of
Richelieu. Proceeding through
the gardens and past the pond,
turn right to exit by rue
Guynemer, and crossing rue
d'Assas turn down rue Vavin.

Le Select

A short walk to the end of rue
Vavin leads you onto
Boulevard Montparnasse, and
Le Dome is on the far side
slightly to the left. Along with
Le Select, La Closerie, des Lilas and La Coupole, Le Dome is one

of a group of cafes in Montparnasse often frequented by Joyce, Beckett, Hemingway and Fitzgerald in the Paris of the Twenties and Thirties.

Nearby is rue Delambre, another of Joyce's favourite haunts. At this point it is perhaps time to stop for a well earned break at one of Montparnasse's many cafes, bearing in mind that a lengthy stay could prove expensive as along the major boulevards a demi (half pint) will set you back about 5 euros. Of course it is always less expensive to consume one's beverage standing *au comptoir* (at the counter).

Once refreshed it is time to continue retracing the steps of Joyce and a stroll along Boulevard Raspail for six or seven minutes will take you to the Metro of Notre Dame des Champs. To the left, the College Stanislas may often have reminded Joyce of his brother, Stanislaus.

Taking the Metro three stops (direction - Porte de la Chapelle) alight at rue du Bac. Just around the corner from the Metro and across Bd. St Germain is the church of St Thomas Aquinas - Joyce was quite an authority on Thomist theology - and at the back of the church in rue Montalembert are the offices of Editions Gallimard, who in 1930 printed the French edition of *Ulysses*.

Not far from here if you have time is the Hotel Lenox, 9 rue de l'Universite, where Joyce and his family stayed on arriving in Paris in July 1920 before moving to  their first apartment in rue de l'Assomption. If you wish to make an extended detour from the main itinerary, the Quai Voltaire and the Port des Saints Peres are quite close with views over the river to the Louvre.

Turning back (from rue Montalembert) towards the Metro rue du Bac proceed along rue de Grenelle to the Mairie of the 7th where Joyce would have conducted his local business during his five year stay at Square de Robiac, his longest place of residence in Paris and perhaps where he spent his happiest years there.

The rue de Grenelle being one of Paris's seriously long streets, it might be better at this point to take the No. 69 bus from Grenelle - Bellechasse to Square de Robiac alighting at Bosquet - Grenelle. The ride will take you past the spectacular Place des Invalides with its ancient copper green cannon situated outside the Musee de l'Armee, and along the rue de Grenelle once more past the Lutheran Evangelical Church of St. Jean, (behind which lies the Student Union of the American University of Paris), to your destination, Square de Robiac - where Joyce and his family lived for over five years from 1925 - 1930. The rather severe modern building at the end of the cul de sac is slightly softened by a trellised wall/miniature garden at its foot. In the nearby rue Cler there is a typical Parisian street market with several cafes. From Square de Robiac, a quiet residential square off rue de Grenelle, it is a five or six minute walk to the nearest Metro - either Latour Maubourg back along rue de Grenelle, or Ecole Militaire straight down Avenue Bosquet.

James Joyce

James Joyce (1882-1941), écrivain irlandais. 1934.

Crédit photographique:
© Studio Lipnitzki / Roger-Viollet

ITINERARY V: VILLA SEURAT - RUE DELAMBRE -
BIBLIOTHÈQUE Ste GENEVIEVE - RUE
DES IRLANDAIS

SCENARIO: It is summer 1932 and the Parisian Police are
raiding hotels throughout the city following the
assassination of the Prime Minister Paul
Doumer by a White Russian immigrant called
Gorgulov. Not having a *Carte de Sejour*
Beckett leaves the Hotel Trianon where he has
been staying to take temporary refuge with the
painter Jean Lurcat in his flat in Villa Seurat,
near the reservoirs de Montsouris.

Needing to leave Paris and go to London for
the time being, Beckett goes to see Edward
Titus, proprietor of *This Quarter* in rue
Delambre. Titus agrees to publish Becketts
translation of Rimbauds *Le Bateau Ivre* (The
Drunken Boat) in the autumn edition of his
prestigious literary magazine for a sum of 700
francs.

Leaving rue Delambre, Beckett journeys to the
Bibliothèque Ste Genevieve, near Pantheon, to
check some literary references before returning
to Villa Seurat and packing for London.

SUMMARY: Start of Itinerary:
Alesia (M) - Ligne 4

8 - 10 min. walk to: Villa Seurat

5 - 6 min. walk to: Rue Marie Rose

5 - 6 min. walk to:	Ave. du General Leclerc
7 min. bus ride (No.68) to:	Vavin (Bd du Montparnasse)
2 min. walk to:	Rue Delambre
5 min. walk down:	Rue Delambre
5 min. walk back up:	Rue Delambre
Short coffee break:	Montparnasse Café
10 min. walk down:	Boulevard du Montparnasse to Avenue de l'Observatoire
7 - 8 min. bus ride (No.38) to:	Rue des Ecoles
8 - 10 min. walk to:	Bibliothèque Ste. Genevieve
8 - 10 min. walk to:	Rue des Irlandais (Centre Culturel /Irlandais)
DURATION:	About 1½ - 1¾ Hours

ITINERARY

The Itinerary begins at Alesia Metro, the penultimate stop on
Ligne 4, direction Porte D'Orleans. It is about a 10 minute walk
along rue d'Alesia to Villa Seurat turning right at rue de la Tombe
Issoire. Proceeding along rue d'Alesia the interesting bookshop
the Librairie Ithaque lies on the right. Villa Seurat is the third
turning on the left down rue de la Tombe Issoire. This quiet cul de
sac in a little known part of Paris is named after the painter
Georges Seurat, and in 1932 was the street in which Jean Lurcat, a
painter and friend of Tom MacGreevy, lived. Later in 1948 Lurcat
was to design the Apocalypse Tapestry and also in 1957 The Song
of the World Tapestry (completed in 1964).

In the summer of 1932 Beckett was just 26 and had been staying
at the Hotel Trianon where he began working on his novel *Dream
of Fair to Middling Women*. Earlier in the year he had been invited
by Eugene Jolas to be a signatory to the 'Poetry is Vertical'
manifesto published in Jolas's transition. A short story *'Sedendo
et Quiescendo'*, some of whose themes would later reappear in
Murphy, had also been accepted for publication in *transition*.
Generally, things were looking up for the young writer.

However, as Deirdre Bair comments in her groundbreaking
biography, Beckett knew he could not put off going to Dublin
much longer and, as often in life, events took a turn which
accelerated the inevitable. The Paris police decided to initiate a
complete check on all foreigners staying in Paris following Paul
Doumer's assassination in May 1932. The trawl, particularly of
hotels, continued throughout the summer and Beckett's anxiety
can be imagined, as he travelled around Paris still not having the
return fare to London or Dublin and in constant danger of being
asked for his papers by an over enthusiastic police officer. But he
had an ace up his sleeve in that he had completed a first draft
translation of Rimbauds *Le Bateau Ivre* which he took to Edward

Titus the proprietor of *This Quarter* [in rue Delambre].

To reach rue Delambre from Villa Seurat it is possible that he may have crossed rue de la Tombe Issoire and turning left taken the first right down rue du Douanier Rousseau and then continued along rue Marie Rose with its striking Franciscan Monastery on one side. Then crossing rue Sarrette and proceeding up rue du Loing, rue d'Alesia and Avenue du General Leclerc lie ahead.

The No. 68 bus, direction Place de Clichy, can be caught at the southern end of Pl. Victor Basch on Avenue du Gen Leclerc. It is a comparatively short bus journey to Vavin Montparnasse passing on the way through Denfert Rochereau, the location of the Parisian Catacombs - ossuaries dating back to 1785. After alighting, cross Boulevard Raspail and rue Delambre lies to the left. Delambre (1749 -1822) was an astronomer who prepared tables that led to the location of Uranus. He also wrote and published *Le Base du Systeme Metrique* in three volumes between 1806 and 1810. A crater on the moon is named after him. On a more contemporary note No. 11 rue Delambre is the location of the Rosebud, a bar much frequented by Beckett in his later days in preference to the main cafes on the Boulevard du Montparnasse. Literary tourists wanting a drink in the Rosebud will find that they have to wait until later in the day as the bar / restaurant only opens at 7pm. Just opposite the Rosebud there is an excellent example of a Parisian fishmongers which is open all week long except for Sunday afternoons and Monday mornings.

Returning to the thirties, Becketts translation of Rimbauds '*Le Bateau Ivre*', a highly imaginative poem in which a boat is personified and which gives us an account of its various voyages, is itself lyrical and highly original. Beckett at this stage in his life was naturally interested in and fascinated by Rimbaud, The *enfant terrible* of modern French poetry.

Having walked up rue Delambre and then back again to the Vavin
end, a virtual galaxy of famous Montparnasse Cafes is to be found
just round the corner in the main Boulevard du Montparnasse. Le
Dome, La Rotonde, La Coupole and Le Select all lie in close
proximity to each other and this may be the opportune moment for
a coffee break. Just across the Boulevard, in the rue de la Grande
Chaumiere, La Villa des Artistes occupies at No. 9 the site of the
former Hotel Liberia, where Beckett recuperated in 1938
following his stabbing by a drunken passer by after a visit with
friends to a cinema. The lady who had the presence of mind to call
an ambulance that evening was Suzanne Dechevaux-Dumesnil,
who later visited Beckett as he recovered in hospital. Suzanne was
subsequently to become his life long partner and they were
married in 1961.

Walking down the Boulevard du Montparnasse there are a number
of good bookshops on each side of the boulevard. The bus stop for
the No. 38 to take us along Bd St Michel is on the right of Avenue
de l'Observatoire near Port Royal Metro. On the other side of the
Avenue, Rude's statue of Marshall Ney, shot in 1815, is
surprisingly lifelike. Nearby is the Closerie des Lilas - another of
the famed 1920s and 1930s Montparnasse *Cafés Litteraires* ...and
Hemingway's favourite. In *A Moveable Feast* he writes 'but the
Closerè de Lilas was such a fine place to write and so convenient
that it was worth the risk of being bothered'.

The Avenue de l'Observatoire lies directly along the line of the
old Paris meridian and is 2° 20' 14" east of Greenwich - a distance
of just over 100 miles / 160 km. At a latitude of 48° 50' Paris lies
about 187 miles to the south of London and is 212 miles distant as
the crow flies, about the same as London to Lancaster. The
Longitude Bureau itself is now in the Institut de France building,
close to the Pont des Arts.

The bus journey up Boulevard St Michel to rue des Ecoles is only a matter of 6 -7 minutes. In a distance of just under a mile the bus passes the Luxembourg gardens to the left and academic Europe's most concentrated area of learning to the right. The Sorbonne and its associated universities, ecoles, and instituts are extended over an area of about a square kilometre. Founded by Robert de Sorbon and St Louis, the king at the time, the Sorbonne first opened in 1253 to cater for the educational needs of 16 poor students. It was to become the main centre of theological study in France until the Revolution, and in the 100 years war was to side with the English and Burgundians and actually provided Joan of Arc's chief prosecutor, Bishop Pierre Cauchon, at her trial in 1431. Its theological faculty also encouraged Philip the Fair in his suppression of the Templars in 1307, by issuing a condemnation of their order.

Alighting at Les Ecoles and turning back down Bd. St Michel, Place de la Sorbonne is on the left. Turning right into rue Victor Cousin, and taking the first left along rue Cujas, the Bibliothèque Ste Genevieve lies on the left on the north side of the Pantheon. The library is situated to the front of St Barbara's College and dates back to 1850. Ste Genevieve, the patroness of Paris, has her shrine in the nearby St Etienne du Mont where some of her relics survive following their exhumation in 1793. It is possible that Joyce may have attended St Etienne du Mont on special occasions as he liked the singing and because, as he once remarked, the Catholic liturgy and ritual represented the oldest mysteries of humanity.

Joyce, who in the 1920s lived nearby in rue du Cardinal Lemoine, often used the Bibliothèque Ste Genevieve where it was (and still is) necessary for readers to obtain a ticket before being allowed access to the books. En route to rue des Irlandais his old address at No 71. rue du Cardinal Lemoine can be reached by taking the rue Clovis exit from the Place Ste Genevieve, and then after crossing rue Descartes - no doubt a fascinating street for Beckett in 1932! -

the rue du Cardinal Lemoine is first on the left. Outside No. 71 there is a plaque to Joyce who is controversially described as an *ecrivain britannique d'origine irlandaise* (see Parisian Odyssey or Parisian Oasis? p.102) and also to Valery Larbaud, the poet, essayist, and hugely influential critic whose plaque reads:

Valery Larbaud (1881 - 1957)
Poete, Romancier, Essayiste, Traducteur vit ici 1919 a 1937.

Joyce was introduced to Valery Larbaud by Sylvia Beach shortly after his arrival in Paris. Larbaud provided a significant boost to Joyce's highly experimental and original *Ulysses* with his enthusiastic support for the novel writing 'with *Ulysses*, Ireland makes a sensational return into the best European literature'!

After visiting No. 71 rue du Cardinal Lemoine (please refer back to Itinerary I) a short walk back up the hill leads to rue Thouin on the right. Rue Thouin then leads into rue de l'Estradapade and rue des Irlandais is the second turning on the left. The Irish Cultural Centre (Centre Culturel Irlandais) is at No. 5 and is based in the old Irish college building. The centre occupies the front of the building and needless to say amongst its many resources, including an excellent Mediatheque, there is a good collection of the works of James Joyce and Samuel Beckett.

Springtime in Paris   © Joanne O'Brien

ITINERARY VI: A BECKETT WALK IN CHELSEA
A 'guest' London itinerary by Tony Murray.

SUMMARY:	Start of Itinerary: 48 Paultons Square
10 min. walk to:	'The Six Bells', King's Road
5 min. walk to:	World's End Bookshop, King's Road
10 min. walk to:	34 Gertrude Street
10 min. walk to:	Edith Grove
10 min. walk to:	Cheyne Walk
10 min. walk to:	Albert Bridge
15 min. walk to:	Sub-tropical Gardens, Battersea Park
20 min. walk to:	Cheyne Gardens
20 min. walk to:	Picasso Cafe, King's Road
DURATION:	About 2 - 2½ hours.

ITINERARY

The walk begins at 48 Paultons Square where Samuel Beckett's close friend Thomas MacGreevy found him rooms in December 1933. Paultons Square runs south from the King's Road and can be reached by bus (numbers 11, 19, 22, 211 and 319) from Sloane Square tube station (District and Circle lines). After his father's death the previous summer, Beckett became deeply depressed and decided to leave Foxrock to seek help through psychotherapy in London. This was not the first time Beckett had moved to London. He had spent an unhappy three months in the city, lodging in a boarding house near King's Cross, during the sweltering summer of 1932. His second sojourn here was somewhat happier, although only marginally. The presence of MacGreevy, who only lived around the corner meant this time he was less lonely having somebody to accompany to galleries, or to share a drink with and confide in.

Leave Paultons Square and turn left into the King's Road. You will pass a pub called Henry J. Bean's Bar on your left. In Beckett's day it was called the Six Bells, and was one of the local hostelries frequented by the two young Irishmen. Continue westwards along the King's Road until the road bends round to the left. Here you will find the World's End second-hand bookshop, which takes its name from this corner of Chelsea and is worth a detour if you have the time to spare. Beckett's only poem to feature locations from his time in London is '*Serena I*' which was published in *Echoes Bones,* one of the original copies of which was annotated by the writer with the words 'London / World's End'. Although the location does not appear in the actual poem, it seems an appropriate reference given the mood of the poem and Beckett's general state of mind whilst living in the city! On the opposite corner of the kink in the road at number 430 is where in 1976, a shop associated with the punk rock band the Sex Pistols was located, led by London Irish punk rocker Johnny Rotten (a.k.a. John Lydon).

Once the road straightens out again, cross over and head straight up Limerston Street, a side road on the right. After about 200 metres, turn left into Gertrude Street. Number 34 was where Beckett moved in September 1934 after returning from a vacation in Dublin and continued to reside until he finally left London in December the following year. He lived in a large bed-sitting room in 'digs' run by an ageing couple, Mr and Mrs Frost. 'Queenie' Frost as the landlady was known was originally from Athlone. She was a good deal more hospitable than Beckett's previous London landladies and became as he later described her, "a mother on draught". Beckett endured the harsh winter of 1934-5 here and his room at number 34 became the inspiration for the one he invented for Celia and Murphy in Brewery Road,

The room was large and the few items of furniture were large. The bed, the gas cooker, the table and the solitary tallboy, all were very large indeed. Two massive un-upholstered armchairs, similar to those killed under him by Balzac, made it just possible for them to take their meals seated... The vast floor area was covered all over by a linoleum of exquisite design, a dim geometry of blue, grey and brown that delighted Murphy because it called Braque to mind. (p.40)

The manuscript of '*Sasha Murphy*', as his new novel was first entitled, was started at Gertrude Road, on 20 August 1935. He worked intensely on it for the rest of the year. Beckett records in his letters how he used to watch an elderly man who lived opposite feeding the birds until one day he died of a seizure. The story of his death is incorporated into *Murphy*, only in much more elaborately plotted form. Locations close to his lodgings appear in the novel also and Beckett would have noted these assiduously on his many extended walks in the vicinity. Further afield, he regularly visited Hyde Park and Kensington Gardens, where the respective landmarks of the Cockpit and the Round Pond provided key settings for Murphy's philosophical musings. According to one of his biographers Anthony Cronin, there was another reason why Beckett chose to take circuitous walks in the neighbourhood. James Joyce's daughter Lucia was staying in London at this time and was hoping to rekindle the relationship she and Beckett had fostered in Paris. However, by this time Lucia's psychological state had become extremely erratic, bordering on the suicidal, and Beckett preferred to remain as elusive as possible. However, in later years, especially after Joyce's death and the war, he would write to Lucia in her nursing home in Northampton on a regular basis.

Continue to the end of Gertrude Street and turn left into Langton Street. When you reach the King's Road again, you will see the famous World's End pub over the road to your left (another favourite haunt of Beckett's). Turn right and then after about 100 metres, turn left in Edith Grove. As you reach the bottom of Edith Grove you will begin to replicate the journey that Celia makes prior to her first meeting with Murphy one midsummer's night.

She had turned out of Edith Grove into Cremorne Road, intending to refresh herself with a smell of the Reach and then return by Lot's Road, when chancing to glance to her right she saw, motionless in the mouth of Stadium Street, considering alternately the sky and a sheet of paper, a man. Murphy. (pp. 11-2)

'The mouth' of Stadium Street is now closed to traffic, but it is still possible to enter on foot and picture Murphy standing here in his 'aeruginous' (coppercoloured) suit and lemoncoloured bow-tie.

After exchanged glances, Celia continues her journey and we will accompany her along Cheyne Walk "to a point about halfway between the Battersea and Albert Bridges" where she sits down on

a bench. Whilst I can promise there are still benches along this
stretch of the Thames, I cannot guarantee there will be, as there
was for Celia, "a Chelsea pensioner and an Eldorado hokey-pokey
man" to sit between. But perhaps you might conjure them up in
your mind's eye. If you are especially conscientious, you will
have taken your walk here at the same time of day as Celia, i.e.
just before ten o'clock in the
evening. If so, you may hear
as she did, the clock of
Chelsea Old Church ringing
out "grudgingly the hour of
ten". The church itself which
is on the corner of Cheyne
Walk and Old Church Street
was badly bombed during the

Albert Bridge

Second World War, but has thankfully been restored since to its
former glory. At this point we will temporarily part ways with
Celia as she returns the way she came to encounter Murphy once
more, still glued to the same spot in the road!

We now continue along Cheyne Walk until we reach Albert
Bridge, clearly visible up ahead, its lights glittering like those at a
fun-fair - surely the most magical of bridges across the River
Thames. En route you will pass a plethora of 'blue plaques' on the
left-hand side of the road. The first at number 109, is dedicated to
the painter Philip Wilson Steer, a leading light of British
Impressionism at the end of the 19th Century. Next door at number
108, lived the Scottish sculptor John Tweed, a contemporary of
Steer's. Further along at number 98 is the birthplace of the
Victorian novelist Elizabeth Gaskell. In the 1970s, Cheyne Walk
was also the location of secret talks between the British
government and the IRA.

When you reach the bridge, cross to the other side and take the
Albert Gate entrance to Battersea Park directly ahead of you.

N.B. This section of the walk can only be taken during the hours of daylight as the park is closed from dusk to dawn. Upon entering the park take the carriageway immediately to you right and follow it until you come to a turning to the left - take this and then immediately take the right fork past the sports pitches until you come to a crossways. Between where you are standing and the lake are the Sub Tropical Gardens, where the Sunday after their meeting Murphy proposes to Celia.

The moon being at conjunction, he proposed to her in the Battersea Park sub-tropical garden, immediately following the ringing of the bell. [...] Resting on Campanella's City of the Sun, Murphy said they must get married by hook or by crook before the moon came into opposition. (p 12-4)

The City of the Sun incidentally was a utopian novel written in the early 17th century by the Calabrian monk Tomasso Campanella and reputed to be the first ever formulation of a scientificallybased socialist system of government.

After our detour to Battersea Park retrace your steps and cross back over Albert Bridge to Chelsea Embankment. Turn right and then left off the main road into Cheyne Walk. Then take the next left into Cheyne Gardens. This is the street where Beckett's close friend Thomas MacGreevy lived at number 15, which is on the right-hand side as you go up the street. Beckett enjoyed playing piano duets here with MacGreevy's landlady, Hester Travers-Smith who was a practicing psychic and later became inspiration for the character of Miss Rosie Dew in *Murphy*. Beckett's visits here entailed him having to negotiate the formidable army of Siamese cats and Pekinese dogs which scuttled in and out of the large drawing room. He was often invited to the house for Sunday lunch, which is where he met Holmes Ravenhill, a pioneer in medicine for altitude sickness and later in life, a painter.

Continue north along Cheyne Gardens (which becomes Chelsea Manor Street) until after 500 metres, you meet the King's Road once more. Turn right here and about 100 metres in the direction of Sloane Square, you will come to the Picasso Cafe, where you can reward yourself with a well-earned beverage. If you require something more substantial, try the Stockpot at number 273 back down the King's Road towards World's End, which serves some of the best 'value for money' fare in London.

ITINERARY VII: RUE EDMOND VALENTIN – RUE GODOT
DE MAUROY - RUE DE LA GRANDE
CHAUMIERE - MAUBERT MUTUALITE

SCENARIO: The time is late January, perhaps early
February, 1938, and there are snow flurries in
the grey Parisian sky. Beckett is recently out of
hospital following his stabbing earlier in the
month by a drunken passer-by as he returned
home from an evening out at the cinema with
friends. Joyce leaves his apartment in rue
Edmond Valentin to meet some friends arriving
at Gare St Lazare from London via Dieppe.
After their meeting at the station they have
light refreshments in the nearby rue Godot de
Mauroy.

After a short time they go on to Notre Dame de
Lorette to pick up Beckett's friend Alfred
Peron who, some three years later, would enlist
Beckett in the French Resistance. They then
proceed to rue de la Grande Chaumiere, a
street in the sixth arrondissement, where
Beckett has a room in a small hotel. Beckett
now more or less recovered from his wounds is
waiting at the Hotel Liberia and the whole
party continues to a restaurant close to Maubert
Mutualite. They finish the evening in a nearby
café in the proximity of Cardinal Lemoine
Metro.

SUMMARY:	Start of Itinerary Rue Edmond Valentin – corner Avenue Bosquet (Metro Ecole Militaire)
No.80 bus to:	Gare St Lazare

(Joyce would have taken a taxi but we are taking the bus!)

Short walk to:	Rue Godot de Mauroy
Short Metro journey from:	Madeleine Metro to Notre Dame de Lorette: Ligne 12 dir. Pte de la Chapelle
Longer Metro journey from:	Notre Dame de Lorette to Vavin (Metro) for rue de la Grande Chaumiere (Ligne 12 to Montparnasse Dir. Mairie d'Issy then Ligne 4 to Vavin dir. Pte D'Orleans)
No.91 bus from:	Vavin Montparnasse to Les Gobelins
No.47 bus to:	Maubert Mutualite
Short walk to:	Cardinal Lemoine Metro
2 - 3 min. walk to:	Finnegans Wake (rue des Boulangers)
DURATION:	About 2¾ - 3 hours.

ITINERARY

The Itinerary begins in rue Edmond Valentin at the corner with Avenue Bosquet. Joyce lived in an elegant apartment here in the late Thirties. There is a plaque to an Argentinian writer, Ricardo Guiraloes 1886-1927 at one address in the street, but none to Joyce. Near the Avenue Rapp end of the street there is a delightful old fashioned *quincaillerie* (ironmongers). The No. 80 bus can be caught at the junction of Avenue Bosquet and Rapp. The route goes over Pont de l'Alma named after a battle in the Crimean war. There are spectacular views of the Eiffel Tower and of the Seine before the bus proceeds along Avenue Montaigne, across the Avenue des Champs Elysees, and into Avenue Matignon close to the Elysee Palace. Depending on the traffic the journey to Gare St Lazare should take about 12-15 minutes.

The Gare St Lazare, the terminal for Normandy and boat trains from Dieppe and Le Havre, lies at the centre of the trapezoid formed by the rue de Constantinople, the rue de Londres, the rue d'Amsterdam, the rue de Rome and the rue St Lazare. To reach rue Godot de Mauroy from Gare St Lazare necessitates a short walk down rue du Havre, across Boulevard Haussmann, a few yards down rue Auber followed by a sharp right turn into rue des Mathurins where rue Godot de Mauroy is the first on the left. An Irish pub, Molly Malones, is half-way down the street on the right.

From Molly Malones to Madeleine Metro, which lies at the end of the Boulevard de la Madeleine, is perhaps a five or six minute walk. The church of Ste Marie Madeleine is well known for its concerts and is a good example of the neo-classical style so much in vogue in early 19th century Paris. The vast building was completed in 1840 and the Corinthian columns are over 60 feet in height.

Notre Dame de Lorette is only three stops from Madeleine Metro

on Ligne 12, direction Porte de la Chapelle. Beckett first met
Alfred Peron at Trinity (Dublin) where Peron was visiting Reader
in French. Later they renewed contact when Beckett in his turn
came to be *lecteur d'anglais* at the Ecole Normale Supérieure.
Peron became a lifelong friend of Beckett's and in 1941 was
instrumental in recruiting him into the Resistance. Beckett
translated and typed out information about German troop
movements until the network was blown in 1942, when on the
15th August he received the telegram that almost certainly saved
his life warning him of an imminent Gestapo raid. He fled with his
future wife Suzanne Dechevaux-Dumesnil to Roussillon in the
South of France where they remained until 1944. In 1945 he was
to receive the Croix de Guerre. Peron unhappily was eventually
captured by the Gestapo and did not survive the war.

The journey from Notre Dame de Lorette to Vavin (changing at
Montparnasse) takes a little less than half an hour. Beckett stayed
in the inexpensive Hotel Liberia between the autumn of 1937 and
the spring of 1938. It was convenient for Montparnasse and the
Left Bank generally, and only three minutes from Vavin Metro. It
was Beckett's home during one of the most eventful periods of his
life. He convalesced here for some weeks after his release from
hospital following his stabbing on January 7th 1938. The blade
narrowly missed his lung and he was considered to have had a
lucky escape. His assailant later confessed that he did not know
why he had done it. In any event Beckett refused to press charges.
Later in the year (1938) *Murphy*, a bleak but comic novel about a
London bed-sit existence, was published (by Routledge) which
reflected Beckett's increasingly pessimistic view of the human
condition.

The No. 91 bus route from Vavin-Montparnasse to Les Gobelins
passes across the Avenue de l'Observatoire. The Observatoire is
Europe's oldest astronomical institution and the place in which the
dimensions of the solar system and the speed of light were first

calculated. It is also the place where the existence of the planet
Neptune was predicted mathematically before its actual discovery.

Close to the Observatoire lie the Hospital Cochin, l'Institut
Protestant de Theologie, and La Maison D'Arret de la Sante.
Alighting at Observatoire - Port Royal - a short walk down
Avenue de l'Observatoire, rue Cassini, and rue du Faubourg St
Jacques brings one to the Institut Protestant de Theologie on
Boulevard Arago and the adjacent Sante Prison. For many years
Beckett lived in a flat overlooking the grim walls of this prison,
site in the past of many an execution. Now grass can be seen
growing out of the windows of the disused cells, and the
Boulevard St Jacques where Beckett came to live in 1961 is quite
an airy, even cheerful, place. No 38 where Beckett and his wife
Suzanne lived is now sandwiched between a supermarket Franprix
and L'Eglise du Christ Scientist. In 1961 Beckett was at this time
already quite famous and in later years even had to make
appointments with his local barber under an assumed name, M.
Daumesnil.

Proceeding back up rue de la Sante to Boulevard de Port Royal it
is probably not worth catching the No. 91 again for only one stop
to Les Gobelins. The Manufacture des Gobelins is a tapestry
factory and museum which goes back to the 15th century. The No.
47 bus to Maubert Mutualite can be caught in Avenue des
Gobelins. Halfway along rue Monge it passes the Arenes de
Lutece (an old Roman site), and depending on the traffic the
journey takes about eight or nine minutes. The Place Maubert,
(Maubert is thought to be a corruption of Maitre Albert a noted
13th century scholar), is a traditional starting point for
demonstrations in the Latin Quarter and at one time was a place
where forbidden books - and heretics! - were burnt. In the
Maubert Mutualite / Cardinal Lemoine area there are numerous
good restaurants but before sampling them a quick stroll around
the Jardin de Plantes is advised. Founded as a botanical garden in

1626 by Louis XIII the garden is open from dawn till dusk. There is an 18th century maze where in 1734 France's first Cedar of Lebanon was planted by Bernard de Jussieu having brought it in his hat from Syria!

Returning to 1938, Joyce's *Work in Progress*, or *Finnegans Wake*, was finally completed in that year, an eventful one for him as well as for Beckett. He had accomplished his life's work and still had some three years to live before his untimely death in Zurich in 1941. To finish the itinerary, and coming from Cardinal Lemoine Metro, Finnegans Wake pub is a short walk down rue des Boulangers and can be found on the right as the street descends sharply into rue Linne and Place Jussieu.

ITINERARY VIII: RUE DES FAVORITES - LAMARCK
CAULAINCOURT - QUAI DE VALMY -
PLACE D'ITALIE

SCENARIO: It is December 1948 and one of the most
severe winters of the century is about to begin.
Joyce has been dead for almost eight years and
is buried in Zurich. Beckett is in his seventh
floor apartment rue des Favorites (15th arr.).
He is in a state of existentialist immobility and
in considerable gloom. Funds are low and he is
stuck at a crucial stage of *En Attendant Godot*
(Waiting for Godot). He is reflecting morosely
on the lack of response the previous year to his
quite substantial output of *Eleutheria, Molloy*
and *Malone Meurt* (Malone dies) but
determines nevertheless to persevere with his
new drama. It is a struggle however. Outside a
cold drizzle is falling on the grey pavements
below, a true Parisian *pluie fine*. Beckett
decides to go out and puts his raincoat on.

He walks briskly down to Place d'Alleray,
hesitates for a minute or two, then walks up to
Pasteur and resolves, because he had been
thinking that day about prime numbers, to go
17 stops on Ligne 12, direction Porte de la
Chapelle. On the train a blind musician comes
and sits next to him and striking up a
conversation offers him a Gauloise - an event
which plunges Beckett into further inner
turmoil. The 17th stop turns out to be Lamarck
Caulaincourt. Beckett alights and wanders
aimlessly for a while pondering on the
Darwinian hypothesis and Hobbes's dictum

that 'the life of most men is nasty, brutish, and short'. Eventually and by a supreme effort of will he quells the tumult within and sets out more purposefully down rue Custine towards Chateau Rouge, Place de la Chapelle, and Place de Stalingrad. Leaving Pl. de Stalingrad, Beckett walks parallel to the Canal St Martin along Quai de Valmy deep in thought once more. Suddenly he encounters a bearded orthodox priest, Greek or perhaps Russian, who asks him the way in halting French. They discuss the weather and Beckett reveals that he is from Dublin where the weather is even worse! The Greek priest talks about some Irish nuns from a nursing order he had recently met in Marseilles. With a cheerful smile he says *"Quelquefois la pire situation precede la meuilleure...n'est-ce pas? Premier, les nouvelles deprimants et après..."* (sometimes the worse situation precedes the better, don`t you think? First the bad news and then...) and with a conspiratorial shrug of his shoulders he leaves. Beckett suddenly feels a new resolve and a new clarity, someone had to set the situation out starkly after all, others would come later to put a different case.

The rain stops, and with a lighter step Beckett proceeds straight to Louis Blanc (Metro) and thence to Place d'Italie and to a favourite café where he takes out his notebook and begins to write quickly and methodically. Some time later he looks around to find the café almost deserted. He puts his notebook away, pays the serveur for his café allonge and takes the

No.62 bus back to rue Brancion. On returning
to his flat again via Pl. d'Alleray, the concierge
beckons, a parcel from Ireland is waiting.

SUMMARY:	Start of Itinerary: Rue des Favorites (Metro Vaugirard)
Short walk to:	Place d'Alleray
Longer walk to:	Pasteur (Metro)
Metro journey to:	Lamarck Caulaincourt (17 stops Ligne 12 direction Porte de la Chapelle)
Longer walk to:	Pl. du Chateau Rouge (20 minute coffee break)
Short Metro journey to:	Stalingrad (changing Barbes Rochechouart) Lignes 4 and 2
Short walk to:	Quai de Valmy
Short walk to:	Louis Blanc (Metro)
Metro journey to:	Place d'Italie (Ligne 7) direction Villejuif (30 min. coffee break)
No.62 bus to:	Brancion / Vouille
Longer walk to:	Rue des Favorites
DURATION:	About 4 Hours.

ITINERARY

Beckett lived in his flat in rue des Favorites from 1938 to 1961, apart from the 3 years between 1942 to 1945 most of which he spent in Roussillon hiding from the Gestapo and as a Red Cross worker in Normandy. Apparently he was pleasantly surprised to find his flat was still there after the war and very much as he had left it after his hurried flight from Paris in 1942. Beckett's modest 7th floor flat in rue des Favorites in one of Paris's more unpretentious districts and largest arrondissement (15th) allowed him ready access to Montparnasse, Boulevard St Germain, and the Latin Quarter. Coming out of the Metro (Vaugirard) take the rue d'Alleray / rue des Favorites exit (sortie). A hundred yards or so down rue des Favorites on the other side of the street is Le Spicy Home, a pleasant café bar restaurant near where Beckett used to live.

Number 6 rue des Favorites was of course the location of Beckett's 'siege in the room', a period of great creativity in his life between 1946 and the early 1950s. During this time he wrote *Mercier et Camier*, the trilogy of novels - *Molloy, Malone Meurt* and *L'Innommable* (The Unnamable) and of course *En Attendant Godot* (Waiting for Godot). Although he had written poetry in French before the war these were his first major works in French, a language in which at that time for whatever reason his creativity was released with greater abundance.

In point of fact it is unlikely that Beckett suffered writers block whilst writing *En Attendant Godot* which he wrote quickly between the Autumn of 1948 and the Spring of 1949 and of which he said the writing just went from 'head to hand'. To digress very slightly at this point, the idea of *Waiting For Godot* arose, according to John Calder (Beckett's publisher), out of his wartime experiences with Henri Hayden, a Jewish painter and friend, and with whom Beckett hid out in the little village of Roussillon d'Apt

(Vaucluse) after having to flee from Paris. However, what is beyond doubt is Beckett's constant pre-occupation with the human condition; the human predicament of having to fill in the space between birth and death. For Richard Kearney (Beckett: The Demythologising Intellect - *The Irish Mind - Exploring Intellectual Traditions*) Beckett, 'more than any other contemporary writer has succeeded in making philosophy literary and literature philosophical'. Whole tracts of his work are explorations into the philosophical reflection on the human condition. His wartime experiences may have served to deepen this pre-occupation: the day to day struggle for survival, the threat of imminent capture by the Gestapo during his work for the Resistance, and the horrors of war generally, although his radio reminiscence of St Lô - where he worked for the Irish Red Cross

• immediately after the war strikes a positive, almost optimistic note on the human potential for survival in the most testing of circumstances. Increasingly, however, Beckett was to see the human condition as a mess which we are powerless to do much about except wait and suffer and perhaps make our slight, individual dent on the walls of suffering which surround us.

Whereas for someone like Viktor Frankl, (*Man's Search For Meaning*) a light shone in the early morning darkness of another concentration camp dawn, for Beckett, like many post war writers, this life was an 'awful, wretched mess' with no obvious destination beyond the grave, and our best hope was to persevere stoically on and do what little we could to improve the lot of our fellow human beings. According to Frankl a seemingly hopeless, meaningless world could yet be suffused with meaning, suffering could be transcended and each life have its own individual meaning, the discovery of which helps our survival here.

Meanwhile, the Beckett who could write in Imagination Dead

Imagine - 'No life ends and no, there is nothing elsewhere' was also the Beckett who could write so inspiringly of 'that smile at the human condition' in his post war radio speech on the experience of St. Lô, and who could say in *Waiting for Godot* 'the tears of the world are a constant quantity... the same is true of the laugh.' If, for Frankl one could say there is 'a divinity that shapes our ends, rough hew them how we will' and that discovering and working towards our individual end (goal) is what is vital and salvific, for Beckett it is the rough hewing or attempt to hew that is important even though our situation is so mysterious and precarious. We cannot do nothing even though our situation may seem hopeless.

Place d'Alleray at the bottom of rue des Favorites is about a 5 - 6 minute walk. The walk up to Boulevard Pasteur via rue Dutot and rue du Dr. Roux takes somewhat longer - about 15 minutes - and on the way there is an unexpected view of the Eiffel Tower at the corner of rue Dutot and rue des Volontaires. A little further on the right lies the Institut Pasteur. This is very much an area of hospitals, the Pasteur, St Jacques, and Necker. This last was named after Suzanne Necker who towards the end of the 18th century opened a hospice in the former Benedictine monastery of Notre Dame de Liesse. She was a firm believer in plenty of air for her patients but unfortunately the death rate at her hospital was higher than any other in the Paris of the time! Many French streets are named after Pasteur (1822 - 1895) the chemist who first discovered the processes of sterilisation and pasteurisation. The entrance to Pasteur is a typical old style but well maintained Metro entrance, and is almost a work of art in itself.

The Metro journey to Lamarck Caulaincourt takes about 30 minutes. Lamarck Caulaincourt lies in quite an interesting part of the 18th arrondissement on the far side of Montmartre. Only 3-4 minutes walk from the Metro on the corner of rue des Saules and rue St Vincent is the famous vineyard of Montmartre, and the equally famous cabaret of Le Lapin Agile. Originally this 19th century concert café was called Le Lapin a Gill (Gill's Rabbit), but it was rechristened the Agile Rabbit by a new owner in 1903. Another version is that its name arose from a sign La Peint A. Gill (There paints A. Gill). In its time it was regularly frequented by Picasso, Max Jacob, and numbered Verlaine and Renoir amongst its habitués. The museum of Montmartre lies further up the rue St Vincent. At the junction with rue de Mont Cenis a right turn leads to the Basilica of Sacre Coeur. The building of Sacre Coeur began in 1875 after being approved by the National Assembly in 1873, and was finally consecrated in 1919. Its enormous Byzantine bulk crowns La Butte Montmartre and it is one of the three most visited places in Paris along with the Eiffel Tower and Notre Dame.

Bearing left after crossing rue du Mont Cenis and along rue Becquerel - Becquerel 1788-1874 was a renowned physicist - it is only a short walk (and a steep descent down almost vertiginous steps!) to rue Custine and Chateau Rouge - which is probably a good point to stop for a coffee. On the way down rue Custine at the intersection with rue de Clignancourt there is an old school building Ecole Roland Dorgeles with two plaques, one to recall that Paul Doumer (a French P.M who was assassinated in 1932) had been a pupil there and the other to remember 700 young Jewish pupils deported from the 18th Arrondisement between 1942-1944. The plaque's final line urges those passing by never to forget them (ne les oublions jamais). From here it would take about 30 minutes to walk to Pl. De Stalingrad but it is only 3 stops on the Metro (changing at Barbes Rochechouart onto Ligne 2, direction Nation). The journey from Barbes Rochechouart through La Chapelle to Stalingrad is quite spectacular. The Metro passing over the Boulevard de la

Chapelle is on an elevated section. Pl de Stalingrad is where
Paris's least known arrondissement, the 19th, begins and is almost
enclosed between the Bassin de la Villette and the Canal St
Martin.

The Quai de Valmy is named after the battle of Valmy in eastern
France in 1792 where the revolutionary army under Generals
Kellerman and Dumouriez unexpectedly defeated a combined
Prussian, Austrian, Hessian and French Royalist army under the
command of the Duke of Brunswick. Goethe who was present
said 'From this place and from this day forth begins a new era in
the history of the world...' Two days after Valmy the Convention
abolished the monarchy and proclaimed the French Republic.

The Quai de Valmy starts on the far side of the Place de Stalingrad
about 100 metres, perhaps less, down rue La Fayette, on the left.
Rue La Fayette which goes all the way from Stalingrad to Opera
is one of Paris's longest streets - about 3km. The Canal St Martin
is thefinal leg of the Canal de l'Ourcq along which a lot of water-
borne traffic arrives in Paris from Eastern France and Germany. A
customs post lies at the end of the Quai de Valmy in rue Leon
Jouhaux. A church, St Joseph Artisan (St Joseph the Worker) lies
at the Pl de Stalingrad end of the Quai.

To reach the Quai de Valmy take a left turn on coming out of
Stalingrad Metro (Quai de la Seine exit), go past the Rotonde de la
Villette and take a sharp right turn into rue La Fayette. The Quai
de Valmy then lies just to the left after about 50 metres. Towards
the end of the first part of the Quai at the intersection with rue
Louis Blanc there is a short line of poplars just before the bridge.
There is also a large theatre barge more or less opposite. The view
along the canal especially at sunset is quite charming.
Turning back up rue de Faubourg St Martin and rue La Fayette it
is then a direct journey of about 30 minutes on Ligne 7, direction
Villejuif or Mairie d'Ivry, as the line branches at its southern end,

to Place d'Italie. The Place d'Italie is a vast cobble-stoned expanse from which many boulevards, avenues, and rues radiate.

For a coffee break it is perhaps best to walk down Avenue d'Italie towards Tolbiac or perhaps down rue Bobillot towards Pl. Paul Verlaine. The thirteenth arrondissement around Avenue d'Italie, Avenue de Choisy, and Avenue d'Ivry is now the centre of the Parisian Chinese community and the Chinese New Year Festival takes place here each year at the end of January / beginning of February. Of course in Beckett's day it would have been very different. One wonders if in 1948 he would have suspected that as a result of writing *Waiting for Godot* he would 13 years later be living in a spacious new apartment just up the road from Place d'Italie in Boulevard St Jacques, and have a country cottage complete with its own piano on the Marne to boot! Back in 1948 and after so many rejections it must have seemed a very remote possibility.

The No. 62 bus which will take us on to the last part of our itinerary can be caught at the intersection of Avenue d'Italie and rue de Tolbiac or at the intersection of rue Bobillot with rue de Tolbiac. It is then a journey of about 4km along rue de Tolbiac and rue d'Alesia to the stop at rue Brancion, 2 stops past Plaisance (Metro). This is where Beckett would have alighted to walk the 5 or 6 minutes home to rue des Favorites.

ITINERARY IX: BOULEVARD EDGAR QUINET - SQUARE
FERDINAND BRUNOT - RUE SOPHIE
GERMAIN - ALLEE SAMUEL BECKETT -
PARC DE MONTSOURIS

SCENARIO: It is 1952 and late autumn. Beckett, heartened
by the recent publication of *En Attendant
Godot* by Les Editions de Minuit and even
more by the news of its impending production
at the Theatre de Babylone in Boulevard
Raspail, decides to take a long relaxing walk
from Montparnasse to Parc de Montsouris via
Square Ferdinand Brunot, where he pauses to
give directions to some tourists from
Brunswick, rue Sophie Germain and Avenue
Rene Coty.

SUMMARY: Start of itinerary:
Edgar Quinet Metro

3 min. walk to: Cimetiere du Montparnasse (main
entrance)

3 min. walk to: Allee Transversale (12e division)

4 min. walk to: Rue Froidevaux (exit)

4 min. walk to: Rue Daguerre

8 min. walk to: Square Ferdinand Brunot

6 min. walk to: Rue Sophie Germain

65

The Paris of Joyce and Beckett. A Tourist Guide. 3rd Edition.

   - Itinerary IX -

9 min. walk to: Avenue Rene Coty

5 - 6 min. walk down: Allee Samuel Beckett

Cross rue d'Alesia, 4 minutes

Walk up and along: Rue des Artistes

5 min. walk along: Rue St Yves

2 min. walk down: Rue Marie Rose

7 minutes walk back to the
steps (rue St Yves) leading
down to: Avenue Rene Coty

Weather permitting 20 minutes exploration of Parc de Montsouris and side streets off rue Nansouty.

No.88 bus back to: Denfert Rochereau (M), or walk back through park to Cite Universitaire.

DURATION: Approx 1½ hours, or 2 hours if coffee break.

ITINERARY

Edgar Quinet Metro lies roughly half way along Boulevard Edgar
Quinet at the point where rue d'Odessa, rue du Montparnasse, rue
Delambre, and rue de la Gaiete all meet.

Leaving the Metro proceed along the right hand side of Boulevard
Edgar Quinet towards Boulevard Raspail and after 200 yards or so
you will find the main entrance to Cimetiere du Montparnasse.
Just inside the main gates there is an old *tronc des pauvres* (or
poor box) which is now sealed up, but which may still have been
in use during Beckett's early years in Paris. Beckett, incidentally,
was unusually generous. And according to John Calder, his
publisher and friend, his generosity often extended beyond his
friends, fellow writers, and students who sought his help, to
complete strangers and on occasion even to shameless rogues. Just
to the right in Division 20 lies the grave of Jean Paul Sartre and
Simone De Beauvoir. The cemetery is open until 5:30pm in winter
and 6pm in the summer. As you proceed up the Allee Principale
you pass the striking headstone of Maryse Bastie, a French
aviator. Further up on the right lies the grave of Eugene and
Rodica Ionesco.

At the Mont du Souvenir turn left into the Allee Transversale and
Beckett's grave, and that of his wife Suzanne Dechevaux-
Dumesnil who also died in 1989 some months before Beckett, lies
about half way down on the left in the cemetery's twelfth division.
The only words inscribed on the dark grey headstone are their
names and dates of birth and death.

Retracing your steps along the Avenue Transversale cross the
inner circle around the Mont du Souvenir, proceed to the end of
the avenue, and then turn left towards the exit in the cemetery's
south west corner which gives on to the rue Froidevaux and the
Avenue du Maine. Baudelaire, Citroen, Maupassant, Poincare,

Rude and Saint-Saens are also buried in Montparnasse but visiting their graves would be a considerable diversion and some of them are not easily accessible. In fact, the cemetery is full of famous names, from Chess Grandmaster Alekhine, to Porfirio Diaz (President of Mexico), Durkheim, Larousse, Man Ray, Proudhon and Tzara.

Walking along rue Froidevaux you soon come to rue Fermat, a street without any particular features apart from the splendid boulangerie/viennoiserie which lies on its top left hand corner with rue Daguerre and looks as though it belongs to a 1920s poster. Turning into rue Daguerre there is an unusually large accordion shop 'Paris Accordeon' which has a charming notice in the window about the *'piano des pauvres'*. Beckett was of course an accomplished pianist but it is not known whether he ever played the accordion! Rue Daguerre is named after Jacques Daguerre (1787 - 1851), the inventor of daguerreotype and one of the early founders of photography.

As you walk along rue Daguerre the third turning on the right is rue Gassendi. Like Fermat and Poincare, Gassendi (1592 - 1655) was also a mathematician and like Delambre has an area of the moon named after him. A short walk up rue Gassendi will bring you to the two squares, Ferdinand Brunot, recorded on the street sign as an historian of the French language and l'Aspirant Dunand, a young man of the *quartier* who died for France in June 1940 aged 22.

It is quite possible that Beckett may have rested from time to time in one or other or indeed both of these squares which share a quiet corner of Paris. Beckett, may on such a walk have recalled a very pleasant week spent in Brunswick in the mid-thirties whilst on a tour of art galleries in Germany. Square Ferdinand Brunot is almost a park in miniature, and is dominated by a large central plinth supporting a bust of Marianne which proclaims your proximity to the imposing Mairie of the 14th arrondissement just 50 yards away.

In the Square de L'Aspirant Dunand there is also an imposing statue of a bearded man chained to a stake. The statue is in memory of Michel Servet/Miguel Serveto/Michael Servetus. The words engraved on the yellow stone are faded but it is just possible to decipher the phrase 'Gardien du Peuple'. (Guardian of the People). Miguel Serveto was a 16th century polymath of Spanish origin who studied theology and anatomy in Toulouse, Paris and Lyons and was the first person in Europe to discover the function of pulmonary circulation. He is more renowned for his book *Christianismi Restitutio* (the Restoration of Christianity) in which he advocated a return to the simplicity of the Gospels. For his pains he was condemned as a heretic by both the Inquisition and the Calvinists and was finally tried and burnt at the stake with his books chained to his leg in Geneva in 1553 at the age of 42.

Calvin, with whom he had been in correspondence, had asked that he should be beheaded rather than burnt but this was regarded as being too lenient for such a dangerous heretic. He has since come to be regarded as one of Europe's outstanding defenders of the radical search for truth and of freedom of conscience. The square also celebrates Khalil Gibran with the legend: '*Ce square salue egalement le poete et peintre libanais, Khalil Gibran par un cedre du Liban.*'

This may be the time to have a short break for tea or coffee. Nearby, at the corner of rue Mouton Duvernet and rue Boulard, there is a cosy and typically Parisian corner café called Le Flash. After refreshments continue along rue Mouton Duvernet to Avenue du General Leclerc, cross to the other side and almost immediately on your left lies rue Sophie Germain, a short street but full of interesting little shops including one devoted to mediaeval militaria!

Sophie Germain (1776 - 1831) is yet another French mathematician of renown and in her time did ground-breaking work on number theory and Fermat's Last Theorem. Because of her gender she would not have been able to gain admittance to the Ecole Polytechnique in the late 18th century, and she resorted to the stratagem of adopting the identity of a former (male) student, Antoine Auguste le Blanc, in order to get access to lecture notes and problems set by the professors. Her consistently brilliant and imaginative answers soon led to her discovery by the course supervisor Joseph Louis Lagrange who became her mentor. Samuel Beckett may not have been a mathematical genius but he was noted for his obsession with counting, numbers, and very precise measurement. From the sixteen stones counted and recounted in *Watt*, to the grains of sand in *Les Depeupleurs* (The Lost Ones) which decrease by three grains every second year and are increased by two every third year, to the statistical calculation of hours spent on licensed premises in *Krapp's Last Tape* and to the four possible trios all given twice in the highly permutated, geometrical, and precisely sequential play *Quad*, examples of mathematical calculation occur frequently throughout Beckett's work.

After walking down rue Sophie Germain bear left down rue Halle and half way down you come upon an entirely unexpected semi-circle of private houses, each one in a different style, which would not be out of place in an English country village or garden suburb. At the end of rue Halle however a glimpse across the street of the overhead suburban train leaving Denfert Rochereau is a reminder of our central Paris location. On leaving rue Halle and turning right into Avenue Rene Coty (formerly Avenue du Parc Montsouris) one almost at once stumbles upon Allee Samuel Beckett. This is a walk through an impressive line of plane trees which run down the centre of Avenue Rene Coty. The street sign bears the legend:

'Samuel Beckett Foxrock 1906 - Paris 1989 Ecrivain Irlandais
Prix Nobel de Litterature'

Fittingly, in view of Beckett's work in 1945 for the Irish Red
Cross in the devastated Normandy town of St Lo, the offices of
the Chambre Nationale des Services d'Ambulance are situated at
the bottom of the building facing the street sign.

Walking down the Allee Samuel Beckett it takes 5 or perhaps 6
minutes at most to reach the intersection with rue d'Alesia. After
the intersection cross to the right hand side of the avenue and
almost immediately one comes upon the steps leading up to the
rue des Artistes (NB there are not that many steps but they are
quite steep). Follow rue des Artistes to the end where you can
either walk down the corresponding steps back into Avenue Rene
Coty or, if you have the energy, there is an interesting diversion
along rue St Yves to the right. A 5 minute walk along rue St Yves
and then the very short rue du Douanier Rousseau brings you to
rue Marie Rose.

The striking red brick Couvent des Franciscains which dominates
one side of rue Marie Rose is visible all the way from the turn into
rue St Yves, but what is really surprising is the first view of the
other side of rue Marie Rose. A balconied seven storey terrace
stretches along the entire length of rue Marie Rose which is
almost the archetype of a quiet Parisian nineteenth century street.
An air of tranquility, almost serenity, hovers over this quiet and
unexpected backwater. Charmingly, the street's name is explained
by the simple statement on the street sign: *'nom choisi par*
l'ancien proprietaire de terrain' (name chosen by the former
owner of the land).

Returning along rue St Yves back to the steps leading down to
Avenue Reny Coty again you find yourself looking across towards
the unexpectedly large green expanse which marks the beginning

of the Parc du Montsouris. Apparently Napoleon III wanted green spaces in Paris similar to London's. On a fine day this park is worth further exploration and contains many features of interest. Looking down Avenue Reille to the left the overhead railway is still readily visible.

One wonders if Beckett, in 1952 when walking down Avenue Rene Coty towards the park, ever recalled the week or so spent in 1932 at the residence of the painter Jean Lurcat in Villa Seurat in the nearby Quartier des Artistes. Much had changed in that 20 years. From being a struggling young writer of 26 unsure of his direction in life, and having to temporarily leave Paris due to not having a valid *carte de sejour,* Beckett was now a mature writer at the centre of Parisian intellectual life who was about to see his masterpiece, *En Attendant Godot*, being performed for the first time at the Theatre de Babylone (January 1953) in Boulevard Raspail. The long years of struggle, rejection and wartime danger, including his courageous work in the French Resistance, had at last melted away and *En Attendant Godot* was about to burst upon an unsuspecting world where it would go on to become the twentieth century's most significant play, provoking countless debates amongst theatre-goers. It would be performed not only in the main theatres of the world's major cities but also in provincial and suburban theatres, in schools and colleges, in community centres and in prisons. After initial audience bewilderment and rejection it would rapidly go on to entertain, perplex and fascinate theatre audiences worldwide.

It could all easily have never happened had Suzanne, Beckett's partner, not persevered with approaching publishers with this work whose genius she instinctively recognized, had the then financially challenged Les Editions de Minuit not taken it on, and the equally financially challenged Petit Theatre de Babylone not secured a small grant from the French Ministry of Culture for its production, and of course if Beckett himself, at a time of great difficulty and discouragement in his 'siege of the room' period in 1948, had not persevered and tried again. In many ways Beckett's own life was a good example of the *obstination humaine* which according to Alain Badiou is so celebrated in his work. One suspects that there was a lightness in his step as he walked the familiar streets and avenues of the 14th in the autumn of 1952 wryly recalling his tribulations of twenty years before.

Almost directly across from Avenue Rene Coty, which ends here, is rue Nansouty, which goes up along one side of the park. Leading off rue Nansouty are some interesting and pretty cobble stoned streets including rue Georges Braque. At this point it is possible to take the No. 88 bus back to Denfert Rochereau or alternatively walk up rue Nansouty and turn left into Boulevard Jourdan in order to reach Cite Universitaire station. Interestingly the No. 88 goes to rue d'Alleray which is close to Beckett's long time residence in rue des Favorites. But in 1952 this route did not exist, and in any case it is quite likely that Beckett would have kept on walking, perhaps stopping for a *café allonge* at the café on the corner of rue Nansouty and Ave. Reille.

Samuel Beckett

© John Minihan

ITINERARY X: PLACE ST SULPICE - POINT ZERO -
SHAKESPEARE & CO - RUE CLEMENT

SCENARIO: It is a warm Paris afternoon in June 1953 and
Beckett has been listening keenly to the radio
broadcast of the Ireland v. France football
match in a Left Bank café just off one of the
main boulevards. He is just about to finish a
cool *biere blonde* when who should walk in
but Brendan Behan! Behan has been sent to
Paris by R M Smyllie, the editor of the Irish
Times, to report on local French reaction to the
international match which is being played in
Dublin's Dalymount Park.

Having listened to the match in the semi-
luxurious confines of his hotel in the
Luxembourg quarter Behan becomes restless
and decides to sample a real Paris café. After a
short but brisk walk he alights on the same café
as Beckett in Place St Sulpice. To his
astonishment he notices his fellow Dublin
writer seated in a corner of the crowded café
whose disgruntled patrons are coming to terms
with an Irish victory. Above the animated post
match conversation Beckett is equally startled
to hear an exclamation in fluent Dublinese:

"By the holy Sam, sure you're a sight for sore
eyes!"
"No more than yourself, Brendan" is Beckett's
reply.

Over a couple of beers the two writers compare
notes on the match won by Ireland because,

according to the French commentator, the
'Dalymount roar' had terrified the French
team. Beckett, like Joyce in his day, is eager as
always to get the latest news from Dublin. He
relegates to the back of his mind his last
encounter with Behan the previous November,
when the younger writer had appeared on his
doorstep in rue des Favorites at the inopportune
hour of 6:30am! After inquiring if Smyllie still
dictated his editorials through a form of plain
chant, Beckett, with his usual courtesy, asks
Behan whether he was still broadcasting for
Radio Eireann on Saturday nights. They
discuss 'Bang-Bang's' latest Leinster House
'holdups' and their conversation broadens onto
literary matters generally and eventually onto
their fellow Dubliner, Sean O'Casey. With
exquisite timing Beckett suggests a walk up to
Pont St Michel to freshen up and Behan readily
agrees.

They proceed up rue St Sulpice, crossing Bd.
St Germain just before Odeon, and a short
walk up rue Danton brings them to the bridge
to the Ile de la Cite. Another short walk leads
them to Place du Parvis Notre Dame where
they examine the bronze plaque in the
pavement which marks Point Zero - the point
in Paris from which road distances to all parts
of France are measured. Brendan Behan, still
only 30, and an accomplished swimmer and
regular diver at Sandycove's forty foot then
asks how deep the Seine is at Pont Au Double.
To Beckett's relief this is purely a factual
inquiry and he proposes a brief visit to the

nearby Shakespeare & Company situated in
rue de la Bucherie.

Leaving the bookshop a little while later,
but not before Behan has recited his Joyce
poem to a group of admiring literary tourists
from Buffalo, they head for rue des Ecoles and
the No. 63 or 86 bus which will carry them
back towards Bd St Germain, rue Clement and
another bar.

SUMMARY:	Start of Itinerary: Café de la Mairie. Place St Sulpice (M. St Sulpice)
9 - 10 min. walk to:	Odeon
7 - 8 min. walk to:	Pont St Michel
3 - 4 min. walk to:	Place du Parvis Notre Dame: Point Zero
4 - 5 min. walk to:	Rue de la Bucherie (Shakespeare & Co.)
Short walk to:	Rue des Ecoles
No.63 or 86 bus to:	Place St Sulpice
Short walk to:	Coolin (rue Clement)
DURATION:	About 1 - 1¼ Hours.

ITINERARY

In June 1953 Beckett was beginning to enjoy international renown
as a result of *En Attendant Godot* which he was then in the
process of translating into English. Behan's best writing to date
had also not been in English consisting mainly of verse in Gaelic
which had appeared in *Envoy* and *Nuabhearshaiocht. The Quare
Fellow, An Giall* (The Hostage) and *Borstal Boy* were yet to be
written. Behan had achieved great fluency in Irish as a result of
long stays in the Kerry and Connemara Gaeltacht in the late 40s.
For someone who was reading the works of Marcus Aurelius at
the age of six perhaps the ability to produce the best Gaelic verse
since the 18th century was not a surprise!

Notwithstanding the mutual mastery of language and power with
words, the background of these two writers could not have been
more different. Samuel Beckett, Foxrock, Portora & Trinity, and
Brendan Behan, Russell Street, national school, and prison, had
already met in the Paris of the late 1940s. By 1948 Beckett had to
a large extent left behind a conventional protestant middle class
public school and Trinity background for the life of an expatriate
writer. Behan was also beginning his journey away from a
passionate and active commitment to working class socialist
republicanism, although he could always have been a character
out of O'Casey's searing plays which brought the reality of
Dublin's tough and tragic inner city life to the stage. Plays like
Juno & The Paycock, and *The Plough and the Stars* were
powerful, punchy, highly controversial and successful. Tragic
situations and desperate dilemmas were uniquely mediated by
O'Casey in a music hall comedy style, and for the first time
Dublin tenement dwellers were given their own ghetto voice on
stage. Although it was 30 years since O'Casey's trilogy, in 1953,
the issues raised had a universal significance and were still
topical.

Although there were, as Behan's biographer Ulick O'Connor points out, genteel and even wealthy influences in his early life, (Stephen Behan, Brendan's father, was a self taught polymath and exceptionally well read), Behan's life up to the early 1950s has been one of continuous hardship, lack of opportunity and, in his membership of the IRA's junior section, life threatening danger. In April 1942 he narrowly avoided being shot by Special Branch detectives in Dublin and in the fraught atmosphere of the Emergency was perhaps lucky to receive only fourteen years on his subsequent capture.

Beckett, coming from an entirely different background and set of circumstances, had also known hardship and frustration, and during the war had also experienced great danger arising from his activities in the Resistance, coming close on more than one occasion to capture and certain death.

By 1953 Behan's career as a writer was beginning to take shape. As well as his published poetry and his programme on Radio Eireann he had also been taken under the wing of the eccentric, resourceful, and charismatic editor of The Irish Times, R.M. Smyllie, who was inspired to ask Behan to cover the French reaction to the Ireland v. France football match. Behan almost missed the match due to his detention at Newhaven because of a still current detention order.

Precisely foreseeing this sort of difficulty Smyllie had in fact given Behan enough money for the airfare, but Behan, being Behan, met a boxer of his acquaintance before the journey and they drank most of the advance! However with the aid of a good lawyer and his brother-in-law in England, Behan finally made it to Dieppe and Paris. Beckett was also keenly interested in sport. At both Portora and Trinity he excelled in rugby and cricket and had shown skill in the noble art of boxing to boot. Famously he went on to play top class cricket for Trinity and is the only Nobel prize winner to be mentioned in Wisden! Interestingly, Albert Camus, one of Behan's other main Parisian contacts along with Sartre and Beckett, had also been a professional footballer before becoming a writer of deeply philosophical novels, playing as a goalkeeper for Algiers.

The Café de la Mairie where the itinerary begins is situated in Place St Sulpice, a short distance away from St Germain. The church of St Sulpice, whose towers can be seen from the nearby Jardin du Luxembourg, was founded in the 12th century to cope with the overflow of worshippers from the abbey of St Germain des Pres. It was substantially rebuilt in the 17th century - the southern façade of the transept being a good example of the 'Jesuit' design.

Inside, in one of the side chapels Delacroix's Jacob wrestling with the angel almost takes up an entire wall. St Sulpice was a 7th century bishop of Bourges in central France. The St Sulpicien Order, set up by the reverend Pére Jacques Olier to provide 'soins des malades et assistance aux pauvres' (care of the sick and assistance to the poor), has been based here since the 17th century. In 1791 the then Cure M. De Pancemont famously refused to take the oath recognizing the civil constitution of the clergy even though the national guard were present in the congregation. The very ornate pulpit he spoke from was the pre-revolutionary gift of the Duc d'Aiguillon du Plessis Richelieu grand nephew of Cardinal Richlieu. In 1791 its ornateness and indeed newness saved it from destruction by revolutionary zealots.

Leaving the café, a few minutes walk up rue St Sulpice leads you to the Carrefour de L'Odeon, where rue de l'Odeon, the original location of Sylvia Beach's Shakespeare and Company, is the central street of the three that meet there. On the way along, an excellent view of the 6th arrondissement's imposing Mairie presents itself at the intersection with rue de Tournon. A few yards further on at the corner with Bd. St. Germain is the memorial to Danton, one of the leading lights of the French Revolution, and who ultimately paid with his head for his opposition to the excesses of Robespierre during the Reign of Terror. On one side of the memorial is an extract from one of Danton's speeches to the Convention Nationale:

'Après Le Pain, L'Education Est Le Premier Besoin du Peuple'
After bread, education is the first need of the people.

On the other side is inscribed Danton's famous phrase:

'Encore de l'Audace et Toujours de l'Audace'
Even more audacity and audacity always.

Crossing the Boulevard rue Danton leads up to Pont St Michel. One can imagine Beckett and Behan as they walked along rue Danton discussing O'Casey's humourous and compassionate portrayal of a world 'in a state of chassis'. Beckett was greatly taken with O'Casey's use of humour and realism in his great 1920s trilogy. In reviewing O'Casey's *Windfalls* in 1934 he had described O'Casey as "a master of knockabout in this very serious and honourable sense - that he discerns the principle of disintegration in even the most complacent solidities". These processes of disintegration in the lives of O'Casey's characters and the world around them, 'the dramatic dehiscence of mind and world asunder', were to be very much part of Beckett's own later dramatic work e.g. *Happy Days*. Behan, in contrast, was not so much influenced as already immersed in the same Dublin socialist republican tenement world which O'Casey so vividly portrayed and brought to life. Due to a literary gift developed in jail, where he could escape the temptation of alcoholic over indulgence, he had re-armed himself with that mind bending Dublinese so faithfully depicted by O'Casey and earlier by Joyce. Whenever the occasion demanded he could dip in to his tremendous repertoire of songs, stories and sketches and reproduce them with a 'Russeller' gusto all of his own.

Beckett although coming from an affluent Dublin suburb did however share a protestant background with O'Casey, and later in the 1950s was so upset by the attempted censuring of O'Casey's *'Drums Of Father Ned'* by Archbishop McQuaid that he withdrew his own work from An Tostal literary festival in protest. Rue Danton soon leads into Place St Andre des Arts and Place St Michel. At this point on the walk three iconic Paris landmarks come into view - the classic entrance to St Michel Metro, a tremendous sudden view of Notre Dame, and the huge statue of St Michael with fountain beneath. Dedicated Joyceans may recall the references in *Ulysses* to Boul' Mich at this point. Crossing Pont St Michel the stern legend on one side of the Palais de Justice strikes the eye:

'Gladius Legis Custo'
The sword is the guardian of the law.

The Pont St Michel, built in the reign of Napoleon III in 1857, also has a plaque in memory of the many Algerians killed in the bloody suppression of a peaceful demonstration (17th Oct 1961). Seventeen years earlier in August 1944, the whole St Michel area was the scene of an intense battle between the French police and the still occupying Nazi forces. There are many plaques in the area to fallen *'gardiens de la paix'*.

At this point, proceeding along the right bank, the massive bulk of the Prefecture de Police looms on the left. Reaching the Place du Parvis N.D. The Hôtel Dieu lies on the left. Still functioning this was the first hospital in the city opened in 651 by Bishop St Landry. A plaque records its origin. Born out of religious initiative it was a symbol of charity and shelter. It was rebuilt in 1877 and many medical pioneers worked, taught and researched in the hospital.

Pont St Michel links the Left Bank with the Ile de la Cite, and turning right on the other side of the bridge a short walk along Quai du Marche Neuf, (overlooked throughout its length by the Prefecture of Police), leads to the Place du Parvis Notre Dame. It is here that the bronze star lies in the pavement across from the cathedral's main entrance which marks Point Zero des Routes de France (Point Zero of French Roads) - the point from which all distances in France from Paris are measured. The actual bronze star-shaped plaque is surprisingly modest and lies in the ground about 40 metres from the Cathedral's main entrance. One can imagine Beckett calculating the distance from Brest to Strasbourg (1079km), or Le Havre to Nice (1130km), and Behan demanding to know how many kilometres it was to the nearest bar! Both Beckett and Behan like Joyce before them were fond of a pint. Interestingly, all three had prodigious memories and could recite whole reams of verse, if in the mood, on request!

In June the Cathedral de Notre Dame de Paris, the most visited site in Paris if not in France, would be full of visitors. Beckett may have recalled Anatole France's remark about the cathedral "as heavy as an elephant, as light as an insect" and would probably have had its main dimensions (130 metres long, 48 metres wide and 35 metres high) at his fingertips. For the more intrepid literary tourist, guided tours of the cathedral set out daily from around 9:30am from the north tower's rue du Cloître entrance. The tours go on all day up until 18:30 in summer and 17:30 in winter, and for those fit enough include a climb of 387 steps to the top of the towers from which a tremendous view of the city unfolds. In June, July and August there are also nocturnal tours, or 'nocturnes'.

Leaving Notre Dame, Shakespeare & Co. (the Continents' most well known English language bookshop) can be accessed by crossing Pont Au Double and walking a short distance down rue de la Bucherie, possibly so named because it was the street in which *bûches* (logs) were collected or stored for the burning of

heretics at the nearby Place Maubert! Opened after the war by
George Whitman it is not connected to the original Shakespeare &
Company owned by Sylvia Beach, although she did eventually
give the right to the name Shakespeare and Company to George
Whitman, which was closed during the war after Miss Beach
refused to sell her last copy of Joyce's *Finnegans Wake* to a
German officer. In the post-war years, and particularly in the 50s,
it would not be unusual for writers such as Allen Ginsberg and
Jack Kerouac to meet here before heading off to Le Gentilhomme
in nearby rue St Andre des Arts, now Corcorans - a popular Irish
pub.

Behan's poem of gratitude to Joyce was written in Gaelic in 1948
and entitled '*Thanks to James Joyce*'. The poem recalls bars in rue
St Andre des Arts and records the poet's debt to Joyce for the
many free drinks - Pernod and Calvados are singled out for special
mention - he had earned through explaining Joyce's work to
puzzled post war Parisians and visitors to Paris. Behan was also a
mentor on matters Joycean for many GIs on leave or demobbed in
post war Paris and indeed in Dublin where many ex GIs had
enrolled in courses at Trinity. Open from noon to midnight the
bookshop has a large collection of new and second hand books.
For many years the almost monastic tradition of allowing
impecunious writers and students of literature to stay here held
sway, provided they helped a little in the daily running of the
bookshop.

The No. 86 bus back to the St Germain Des Prés Quartier can be
caught by walking up rue St Jacques and turning left into rue des
Ecoles. Alighting at Place St Sulpice again, the 'Coolin', an Irish
pub, can be reached by walking back to rue Mabillon and going
up this street. Rue Clement is the second turning on the right.
Coolin was perhaps Behan's favourite song and on one famous
occasion in Dublin he brought a whole street to a stop with his
heartfelt rendering of this traditional ballad. Beckett also had a

great ear for music and whilst not a singer in the mould of Behan
or Joyce - both tenors - he was an accomplished pianist and there
is a musical quality about much of his work. Although his
favourite composers were Schubert and Beethoven he also liked
going to music halls on occasion and enjoyed the songs of Jacques
Brel and Georges Brassens.

Brel became popular in Parisian cabarets and music halls in the
1950s. He had a great lyrical talent as exemplified in *Je Suis Un
Soir d'Ete* in which a summer's evening is personified as it falls
on and overlooks a city. He combined this talent in his later work,
especially, with an intense exploration of the great themes of love
and death and of the sense of exclusion suffered by those on the
margins of society. His statement 'in a man's life there are two
important dates: his birth and his death, everything we do in
between is not very important' would surely have appealed to
Beckett.

1953 was in many ways a crucial year for both Beckett and Behan
and marked the beginning of a period of great success for both
writers, leading ultimately to the Nobel prize for Literature for
Beckett (1969) but tragically to the ravages of alcoholism and an
untimely death for Behan (1964). In their different ways both
these Dublin writers, like Joyce before them, faced the human
predicament with great verve, originality, and courage, and en
route contributed to making post-war Paris the fascinating centre
of literature and literary life that it was.

GEORGE WHITMAN

George Whitman who sadly passed away in 2011 had the bookshop in rue de la Bucherie, near St Julien Le Pauvre and Quai de Montebello, as his life project. He acquired the premises just after the war and opened the bookshop, Le Mistral, as it was called then, in 1951 building it up to be a wonderful place for book lovers. The hospitable atmosphere, the support for lesser known writers, students and volunteers, extending even to accommodation within the shop in return for a couple of hours of assistance each day, the time given to help customers make that special purchase, made the bookshop an example of all that is good in independent bookselling. In 1958 Sylvia Beach announced over dinner with George Whitman that she was handing over the name 'Shakespeare and Company' to him for his bookshop and in 1964 the bookshop was renamed.

Visiting the shop one afternoon in the late 90s to research this guide, I was startled when George asked me to mind the till for half an hour while he had a break. Of course I obliged. I had only sold one book when he returned some 25 minutes later but what a thrill it was to have been able to put the famous Shakespeare & Company stamp on the title page!

We can only wish George Whitman's daughter, Sylvia, now even more at the helm of this flagship of independent bookshops as it sails through the uncharted or perhaps too well charted waters of e-books and bookstore chains and internet purchasing, and her staff and volunteers all the best. We ask ourselves if scrolling down will ever be quite the same as turning over a page and just thinking about that for a moment realise that there will always be a future for a good bookshop.

For George Whitman may we be so bold to quote some lines from his namesake Walt Whitman's poem, *A Clear Midnight:*

This is thy hour, O Soul, thy free flight into the wordless,
Away from books, away from art, the day erased, the lesson
done...

Away from books perhaps but hopefully not for very long!

LE DEJEUNER ULYSSE

The 'Dejeuner Ulysse' was the idea of Adrienne Monnier, the proprietor of La Maison Des Amis des Livres at no 7 rue de l'Odeon just across the street from Sylvia Beach's Shakespeare and Company at no 12. Before opening her bookshop, Monnier, who loved the world of literature, had been a teacher and then a literary secretary. In the 1920s Monnier and Beach's bookshops, just across the street from each other, became popular meeting points for writers in Paris as well as venues for readings, talks and lectures.

Monnier organised the Ulysses luncheon which was held on the 27th June 1929 to mark the occasion of the completion of the translation of *Ulysses* into French and also a little belatedly to commemorate the 25th anniversary of 16th June 1904, the date on which Joyce set the events of his groundbreaking novel. Earlier in 1921, Jacques Benoist-Michens, an exceptional student of the poet and critic, Valery Larbaud who was an early and influential supporter of Joyce's epic novel, had translated extracts from *Ulysses*, but the translation of the entire work, led mostly by Auguste Morel, was only finally completed in 1929. Morel had been taken on for this mammoth task on the understanding that his work would be reviewed by Larbaud and by Joyce himself. From 1927 onwards he was also assisted, at Joyce's insistence, by Stuart Gilbert.

Monnier hired a bus for the occasion to transport the chosen literary luminaries who included Edouard Dujardin, Leon Paul Fargue, Valery Larbaud, Jules Romains, Philippe Soupault and Paul Valery to the Restaurant Leopold in the small village of Les Vaux de Cernay situated between Versailles and Rambouillet, some 45 km from Paris. The Restaurant Leopold was selected to receive this singular honour 'only because of its name' according to Deirdre Bair in her biography of Samuel Beckett who was one

of the guests at the luncheon mainly through his friendship with
Thomas MacGreevy. Les Vaux de Cernay is mainly known for its
Cistercian Abbey and for the *Historia Albigensis* (History of The
Albigensian Crusade) written by Peter des Vaux de Cernay, a
knight of Simon de Montfort's invading army in Languedoc.

In 1929, however, over twenty literary guests sat down for the
'Dejeuner Ulysse' beginning with *le pate Leopold* which was
followed by four other courses including *les quenelles de veau
Toulouse, le poulet de Bresseroti* and *la salade de laitue mimosa.*
A wide variety of wines, cheeses and liqueurs completed the
menu.

One of the principal guests was Valery Larbaud who had written
the introduction to the French translation and who, in December
1921, had given the crucial lecture in Monnier's bookshop at
which translated extracts from *Ulysses* were first read out to a
French audience. Also present at the luncheon was the novelist
Edouard Dujardin, originator of the stream of consciousness
technique, a debt freely acknowledged by Joyce. In a Europe
fascinated by what were then the revolutionary theories of Freud
and Jung, Joyce remarked that he was interested not so much in a
theory of unconsciousness but more in a theory of consciousness
as always making a pithy comment: there was tremendous interest
in the 'discovery' of the unconscious but still no adequate
explanation of consciousness itself. Joyce had read Dujardin's
novel *'Les Lauriers Sont Coupes'* which had been published as
early as 1887 and this had led him without any help from
psychological theories to an understanding of and enthusiasm for
the immediacy and realism of the stream of consciousness
technique which he then brought to an unsurpassed level of
accomplishment in *Ulysses.*

Other guests included Jules Romains, the founder of Unanimisme
and Paul Valery, the symbolist poet and critic. But, *naturellement,*

the centre of attention, surrounded by family, friends and literary contemporaries was Joyce himself, arguably at the apex of his career and fortune and now a firmly established figure in Parisian literary and intellectual circles as well as a writer of international renown.

The lunch finished a little earlier than anticipated partly because two of the guests, the poet Thomas MacGreevy and a young lecturer in English at the Ecole Normale Superieure, Samuel Beckett, at 23 one of the youngest guests, had both drunk too much to the taste of their older and more sedate fellow diners. Adrienne Monnier took charge, arranged for a speedy photo session and then it was back to Paris on the bus. Not to be denied the two younger men persuaded the driver to stop at several watering holes on an increasingly lengthy return journey which further incurred Monnier's disapproval. Eventually, the young Samuel Beckett was abandoned and the bus continued its journey back to La Maison des Amis des Livres in rue de l'Odeon where, none the worse, the guests disembarked after a memorable day in literary history.

Almost two years later, In March 1931, many of the same guests, including Beckett, reassembled at Monnier's bookshop to attend a *Séance Consacree a James Joyce* which once again she had organised and where the principal speaker was Philippe Soupault on the subject of *Anna Livia Plurabelle*.

AN APPRECIATION of THOMAS MACGREEVY
by Rhiannon Moss.

One figure above all others was influential in Beckett's Parisian
life. The poet Thomas MacGreevy had held the post of lecteur at
the École Normale Supérieure in the year before Beckett arrived
to take the job, and he remained in a similar position for two more
years. The two Irish writers soon began a friendship that was to
become one of Beckett's most important relationships through the
1930s, and which shaped his first experiences of Paris.

MacGreevy has sometimes been a neglected figure in Irish
literature, remembered more for his friendships than his own
work. This has begun to change, and since Susan Schreibman's
edition of his poems (published in 1991) the significance of his
work as one of the first Irish modernist poets has received greater
attention. Beckett was a great admirer of his friend's work, and in
1934 described it as "probably the most important contribution to
post-War Irish poetry."

As well as their shared interest in writing and the arts, MacGreevy
was famously friendly and gregarious, and his outgoing
personality was the perfect complement to the quiet, sometimes
withdrawn young Beckett. Their friendship flourished despite
some differences in their experiences and attitudes. MacGreevy
was born in 1893 in the village of Tarbert, in County Kerry, to a
Catholic and nationalist family (his father was the local policeman
and his mother a primary school teacher), a background very
different from Beckett's prosperous suburban Protestant
upbringing. MacGreevy remained a devout Catholic throughout
his life, and his poetry is marked by a strong sense of faith, even
when dealing with the darkest moments in personal experience
and national history. He and Beckett often debated their differing
views on religion, while always remaining tolerant of each others'
beliefs.

The difference in their ages also had a significant impact. MacGreevy reached adulthood in an Ireland still part of Great Britain. At seventeen he joined the civil service, and after a year working in Dublin moved to the English service in London. During the First World War he worked for the Admiralty before joining the British Army in 1917, and he fought at Ypres and the Somme. The horrific experience of the trenches left a permanent impression and features often in his later writing. It caused a deep disillusionment with the imperial powers and with Britain in particular, and contributed to a commitment to Irish independence that included, twenty years later, support for Irish neutrality during the Second World War.

After being demobbed in 1919, MacGreevy took a scholarship available to ex officers to attend Trinity College in Dublin, where he began writing. He remained in Dublin until 1924, when he moved to London to continue his poetic and journalistic career. In 1927, with a recommendation from his friend TS Eliot, he began his post at the École Normale. He remained in Paris until 1933, and these years were some of the most creative of his life. He was an all-round man of letters, writing critical essays and reviews as well as poetry, which he contributed to journals such as *transition* before publishing his only collection, *Poems*, in 1934. He shared with Beckett a love of the arts, and impressed the younger man with his wide knowledge - Beckett called him a 'living encyclopedia'. His knowledge and experience of Parisian life made him an excellent guide for the newly arrived Beckett, and his contacts among Paris' artistic community meant he was able to provide Beckett with many introductions.

Perhaps the most valuable introduction MacGreevy was able to give to Beckett was to James Joyce. During his first year in Paris MacGreevy had become close to the Joyce circle, providing reading and assistance with his '*Work in Progress*' as well as friendship to the by then famous Irish writer. It seems that

MacGreevy introduced Beckett to Joyce very soon after his arrival in Paris. Beckett recalled the meeting as 'overwhelming', although Joyce was 'very friendly'. Beckett too started helping Joyce with *Work in Progress*, often reading to him and sometimes taking dictation. The three men shared a great deal, but MacGreevy later described a difference in their attitudes to Ireland, perhaps reflected in MacGreevy's friendship with Nora Joyce, which Beckett never shared. He recollected that before his first meeting with Joyce "my feelings were mixed. Of the stories in *Dubliners*, I had found 'The Dead' very moving and beautiful. But then that was not so much a Dublin story. The woman in it came from Galway, from the Ireland outside of Dublin - the Ireland which I belonged to, which Joyce could feel but did not know. Once he said to me something like, "This Ireland that you talk about is strange territory so far as I am concerned. Thirty miles from Dublin and I am lost."

Nora was more my own kind of Irish [...] From [Joyce's] manner when I saw him, I could believe he was putting into practice his theory that the solution for the Irish artist of his time had been "silence, exile and cunning." I was not naturally given to silence, and Sunday after Sunday all through my years as a growing boy, I had heard our parish priest at home quoting Saint Augustine to the effect that open confession was good for the soul. I had had plenty of exile and did not think much of it. And the implications of the word "cunning," except in relation to the technique of art, were unpleasant."

This is revealing about the differences between MacGreevy and Beckett which were to manifest in their future careers. As well as his commitment to his faith, MacGreevy felt a connection to Ireland which Beckett could only problematically share. As Beckett wrote to him after the war in response to MacGreevy's book about the painter Jack B Yeats, in a letter questioning MacGreevy's emphasis on social and political forces, "God love

thee, Tom, and don't be minding me. I can't think of Ireland the
way you do."

MacGreevy's feeling for Ireland meant he could not live his whole
life abroad. After his time in Paris he spent most of the 1930s in
London, where he continued writing as well as lecturing at the
National Gallery until 1941. When the pressure of the war meant
the Gallery could no longer continue its lecture programme he
returned to Dublin where he remained for the rest of his life. He
joined the editorial board of the intellectual Catholic periodical the
Capuchin Annual, and in 1950 became director of the National
Gallery in Dublin. There is sometimes a perception that
MacGreevy's return to Dublin was a time of transition from
cosmopolitan bohemianism to a more conservative nationalism.
This however misrepresents MacGreevy's attitude to Ireland. He
considered no contradiction between a commitment to both
Ireland and Europe, and saw the future of independent Ireland in a
strengthening of connections with the continent. He retained a
deep affection for France in particular (and the respect was
reciprocated - he was made a Chevalier of the Légion d'honneur
by the French government in 1948, and Officier in 1962). His
years in Paris created a love for the country which never waned,
and was the place he was to associate most strongly with
intellectual joy. The 'umbilical hold' he felt Ireland had for him
was however too strong for him to make it, as Beckett did, his
permanent home.

References:

Samuel Beckett, 'Recent Irish Poetry' in *Disjecta: Miscellaneous
Writings and a Dramatic Fragment*, ed. Ruby Cohn (London:
John Calder, 1983), pp.70-76

Hugh J Dawson, 'Thomas MacGreevy and Joyce' in *James Joyce
Quarterly* 25:3 (Spring 1988), pp.305-21

The Paris of Joyce and Beckett. A Tourist Guide. 3rd Edition.
- An Appreciation of Thomas MacGreevy -

James Knowlson, *Damned to Fame: The Life of Samuel Beckett*
(London: Bloomsbury, 1996)

Susan Schreibman, Introduction to *Collected Poems of Thomas
MacGreevy* (Dublin: Anna Livia Press, 1991)

'WHEN DOES JOYCE COME IN?'
Joyce and Hemingway and Shakespeare & Company

Not long after his arrival in Paris in December 1921, Ernest Hemingway made his way to Shakespeare & Company, Sylvia Beach's bookshop newly located in rue de l'Odeon between the Boulevards Saint Germain and Saint Michel and just across the street from her friend Adrienne Monnier's La Maison des Amis des Livres, and boldly asked Beach, 'When does Joyce come in?' To which, she replied 'If he comes in it's usually very late in the afternoon'. Hemingway had heard about Joyce and had read *Dubliners* and in the words of Aubrey Dillon -Malone in his book on Hemingway 'had become entranced like most young turks who sculpted syllables for a living by its poetic rhythms and the ominous air of tension that hung between the lines.'

Like Joyce, Hemingway had come to Paris, the place where, in Gertrude Stein's memorable phrase, 'the twentieth century was', to escape the strict limitations of his homeland. At the early age of 22 on the strength of his earnings from writing for The Toronto Star and with the help of his wife Hadley Richardson's trust fund, Hemingway had made the break from Illinois and arrived in the world's cultural epicentre. Three years previously he had been a volunteer ambulance driver on the Austro - Italian front during the First World War and had been wounded and twice decorated. Now he was about to embark on a remarkable literary career in the citadel of modernism.

Sylvia Beach, if not a mentor like Gertrude Stein, was nonetheless to become one of his guides and mainstays in his new abode. Of Beach, he was later to say, 'she was kind, cheerful and interested and loved to make jokes and gossip. No one that I ever knew was nicer to me.' Beach, of course, had already taken Joyce under her wing, lending him money, cashing his cheques and finally, offering to publish his epic novel *Ulysses* when nobody else would. Beach had met Joyce within days of his arrival in Paris at an afternoon party organised by Ezra Pound, another expatriate American, in his honour at the Neuilly home of the poet, Andre Spire.

Pound who had had the foresight to recommend a Paris stopover to Joyce and more importantly to persuade him to stay there, finding the Joyce family their first Paris flat in rue de l'Assomption, was also to become an important figure in Hemingway's life developing a solid rapport with the young writer from Illinois even to the extent of taking boxing lessons from Hemingway while Hemingway in turn picked up literary tips from Pound's style.

Ernest and Hadley initially stayed in the Hotel Angleterre (44 rue Jacob). The young couple soon found their way round and for Christmas Day 1921 they went to the Café de la Paix in Avenue de l'Opera. In January 1922 they found an apartment at 74 rue du Cardinal Lemoine very close to the Joyces' recent residence at no 71. The two writers were not to meet until March 1922, shortly after the publishing of *Ulysses*, possibly when they were both en route to a conference. They were to become friends, drinking together, often at Harry's New York Bar in rue Daunou near Opera and Joyce was to become one of the few writers that Hemingway did not have a falling out with although Hemingway did once famously remark on 'Joyce and the whole Celtic crew' affecting hardship whilst dining in the most expensive restaurants.

Hemingway was complimentary about *Ulysses* saying that Joyce had produced a 'most goddam wonderful book' and later, after *Ulysses* had been banned in the United States, he came up with an unusual means of ensuring that copies reached eager American readers by persuading a friend in Chicago to move to Canada - where the book was not banned - and to smuggle copies across Lake Ontario to the US stuffed in his trousers! Eventually another friend joined in this literary smuggling run and soon subscribers were able to get their hands on a copy without having too long a wait. Joyce was similarly complimentary about Hemingway's writing, remarking that there was more to his style than people realised. Perhaps also the young American writer owed something to Joyce's development of the 'telegraphic style' - short impactful sentences of pulsating word pictures, a sort of 'literary infra red ray'.

Years later, Hemingway was very depressed by Joyce's death in 1941 but perhaps a fond memory for him was an evening in the company of James and Nora when Joyce asked him if he felt his (Joyce's) work was too 'suburban'. Before Hemingway could reply, Nora remarked that 'Jim could do with a bit of that lion hunting' to which Jim agreed but with the proviso that he wouldn't be able to see the lions with his bad eyesight. Quick as a flash, Nora said, 'Ernest would describe them to you and afterwards you could go up to them and touch them and smell them. That's all you'd need!'

Perhaps the last word should lie with the French novelist Andre Chamson's insightful observation, reported in Virginie Raguenaud's article *Sylvia Beach's Shakespeare & Company: A Mecca For Contemporary Literature,* 'Sylvia carried pollen like a bee. She cross-fertilised these writers. She did more to link England, the United States, Ireland and France than four great ambassadors combined. It was not merely for the pleasure of friendship that Joyce, Hemingway, Scott Fitzgerald, Bryher and so many others so often took the path to Shakespeare & Company in the heart of Paris, to meet there all these French writers. But nothing is more mysterious than such fertilisations through dialogue, reading or simple human contact'. 'Through these fertilisations', Raguenaud writes, 'Sylvia Beach and Adrienne Monnier's two bookshops continued to gently sway the course of modern literature'.

CHASING JAMES JOYCE IN PARIS
By Grace Holtkamp

There are some places in the world that once we have visited call us back in the most peculiar ways. As one of these remarkable locales, Paris holds its own very potent magic for many people. Artists, lovers and socialists come to mind. But not being a member of any of these tribes, I was as recently baffled as those close to me when I announced I was being summoned by some prime mover to Paris. My first visit to Paris being dreadful on account of rain and Parisians, I was perplexed to find myself animated by an acute need to leave my flat in Edinburgh, where my studies were soon to recommence in September, and make my way back, alone, to the City of Light.

If it is not clear already I will make it explicit now that I am not one of those quick thinking and self aware sorts. It was truly, only when I paused, the night before my journey, to consider what book I might bring with me that I saw my copy of *Finnegans Wake* on my desk. And then in true Joycean style, I had an epiphany of sorts. I was going to Paris to mourn James Joyce.

My trip to Paris was a sort of quixotic pilgrimage through which I intended to pay my respects to the great modernist writer. I would travel to the city in which he grew old, went blind, lost his daughter to a mental asylum, worked alongside Samuel Beckett and wrote the book which had come to and still does enthrall me, *Finnegans Wake.* The novel had been my primary occupation all summer and would be the subject of my dissertation in the fall.

Finding oneself alone in Paris, possessing the twin faults of not speaking the language and being an American, is unsettling, even with the aid of Google maps and the superbly helpful staff at the Hotel Le Six (just a few blocks from the Victoria Palace Hotel where Joyce wrote much of *Finnegans Wake).* James Joyce and I had this much in common: neither of us could afford the Right Bank. From biographies and critical writings I knew that Joyce walked miles each day in Paris, down Boulevard Montparnasse, through the Luxembourg Gardens, across the Seine (sister to his beloved Liffey) down the sandy paths of the Tuileries gardens and up the great stretch of the Champs Elysees. Before the Arc de Triomphe James Joyce habitually made his way past the illustrious Pont Alexandre to the smaller, unadorned Pont de l' Alma.

I traced his route and finally stood on Pont de l'Alma with the Eiffel Tower or 'Eyeful Hoyth Entowerly', (as Joyce would call it in *Finnegans Wake*) looming on one side and the brilliance of Pont Alexandre's gilt columns on the other. I had intended to visit the bridge in honor of the man who labored for seventeen years in Paris on a masterpiece that critics have called everything from stillborn to unreadable, to have a moment's silence on a Parisian afternoon, standing where he stood, myself, a foreigner in France as he was, my mind on *Finnegans Wake* as his was.

At the very moment of this solemn obeisance, the very moment of the realization of my pilgrimage, I was confronted by the entirely practical problem of which way to face, that is, which vista of the bridge to turn to. The problem with chasing a ghost is that there are these inevitable practicalities that threaten to deflate the romance of the whole enterprise. I was forced to ask myself the ridiculous question: which way would James Joyce have faced? This was of the utmost importance. If I could not answer it, I would simply be an idle student, grown anxious at the thought of impending autumn, who had fallen in love with an impossible book, and had essentially run away to Paris out of a certain procrastination and possible lunacy.

One side of the bridge affords a remarkable view of a long stretch of the Seine, with the bright dome of the Musee d¬Orsay on one side and the Louvre on the other, with all the luster of Pont Alexandre in the middle. From the other side, the Seine bends abruptly to the left, and what is beyond the river bend is obscured. Noticing the river bend, I was reminded of that very first word in *Finnegans Wake*, of the very first rushed and wending sentence: 'riverrun'. The Seine flows through Paris like the Liffey flows through Dublin, but as the readers of the *Wake* know, the Liffey flows through *Finnegans Wake* as well. The magic of a river bend is that a person can imagine anything at all, whatever we wish for, is just beyond it. Writing throughout all the nights of all the seventeen years a novel that was immediately and ferociously criticised as it was released instalment by instalment, that cost him friends, patrons and his eyesight, in his own peculiar exile from his home country, James Joyce had much to wish for.

It is for anyone to judge, but I decided it was the view of the river bend that brought Joyce habitually to Pont de l'Alma. I have doubts about my conclusion, and consequently about the real nature of my trip to Paris. But at this point I might defer to Joyce himself - it would only be right - who reminds us, 'Mistakes are the portals of discovery.'

Chasing James Joyce In Paris
Grace Holtkamp
Copyright 2011

PARISIAN ODYSSEY OR PARISIAN OASIS?
Joyce's Moves in Paris 1920 - 1939

Louis Gillet, a Parisian friend of Joyce's, once claimed '…one cannot say Joyce settled in Paris for he continued wandering between Passy, le Gros Caillou, Montparnasse and Grenelle.' Gillet went further: 'I never saw him in the same lodgings for more than six months, his page in my address book is filled with numerous erasures.' On the face of it it is hard to disagree with Gillet's assessment of Joyce's constant moves around Paris which seemed to mirror his father's constant moving around Dublin in his childhood and youth. Between July 1920 when Joyce and his family arrived in Paris from Trieste and December 1939 when they left Paris to spend Christmas in the relative safety of St Gerand le Puy in the Auvergne they lived in no less than 17 different addresses in the city.

But on further inspection, Gillet's view of Joyce's tendency to up sticks and move and other writers' attribution of nomadism to Joyce seem exaggerated. When Joyce's moves are examined more closely we see that they are often a response to some external pressure such as a lease expiring and the landlord wanting the apartment to be vacated or a friend needing back an apartment that had been loaned or a move could occur because of an exceptional family reason as when the Joyces left Paris for London in 1931. In fact, during the 19 years and 3 months the Joyce family was in Paris, over 12 of those years were spent in just 3 addresses: Square de Robiac (almost six years), rue Edmond Valentin (four and a half years) both in the seventh arrondissement and rue Galilee (almost two years) in the eighth.

Arguably, the years spent in Square de Robiac, 1925 - 1931, were the Joyce family's happiest and most stable during their time in Paris. Joyce had become an established writer of international renown and despite his perennial eye problems was making steady progress with his *Work in Progress, Finnegans Wake*, his family had become accustomed to Parisian life and his daughter, at least until 1930, had not yet developed the devastating and bewildering symptoms of schizophrenia that characterised her life for most of the nineteen thirties. Despite their relative happiness in this quiet *quartier* of the seventh with its local street market in rue Cler and handy Metro Ecole Militaire the forthcoming marriage of Giorgio Joyce to Helen Fleischmann in 1931 necessitated Joyce and Nora regularising their own union. They decided to do this in London and were thus required to spend three months there prior to their registry office marriage in Kensington in July 1931.

The first abode of the Joyce's in Paris was the Hotel Lenox in rue de l' Universite, an address they were to stay at on two subsequent occasions in 1920 and 1921. Their second Paris address was the small flat in rue de l'Assomption in Passy which was put at their disposal by Madame Bloch - Savitsky, a friend of Ezra Pound's in July 1920 which served to accommodate the family for those vital first months up to November 1920. The rue de l'Assomption is named after the Convent of the Ladies of the Assumption, a religious order founded by St Marie Eugenie de Jesus whose mother house and chapel is half way up the street.

Perhaps one of the most well known of Joyce's Paris addresses is no 71 rue du Cardinal Lemoine where he and his family stayed for a comparatively short five months from June to October 1921. The comfortable apartment, lent to Joyce by the poet and essayist, Valery Larbaud, just downhill from Place de la Contrescarpe in the 5th arrondissement described lyrically by Hemingway in *The Snows of Kilimanjaro* as the place of drunkards and sportifs where flowersellers dyed their flowers in the street, or just uphill from Cardinal Lemoine Metro and situated within the confines of a courtyard and accessed by almost a semi rural path, was the address at which Joyce finally completed *Ulysses*.
Perhaps because of this, it is the only one of Joyce's addresses in

Paris which actually has a plaque, only recently erected, to the twentieth century's most original and influential writer describing him controversially as an *ecrivain britannique* and attempting to soften or qualify this appellation or misappellation if you will, with the rider, *d'origine irlandaise.* Although Joyce, like many Irish people before 1921, held a British passport throughout his life for reasons of his own, he is universally regarded as an Irish writer, much as Dylan Thomas or Robert Burns would be regarded primarily as Welsh or Scottish writers and would have certainly regarded himself as such. In fact, in the days before the Euro his portrait even adorned Irish banknotes! Elsewhere in Paris, Shaw (rue George Bernard Shaw - 15th) and Beckett (Allee Samuel Beckett- 14th) are both described unequivocally as *ecrivains irlandais.* Indeed, Joyce himself, is also so described in Jardin James Joyce in the 13th arr. near Quai de la Gare.

The Victoria Palace Hotel in rue Blaise Desgoffe (Metro - Placide) close to College Stanislas, rue de Rennes and Boulevard du Montparnasse became the Joyces' base for flat hunting in August 1923 following their move from Avenue Charles Floquet where they had spent a pleasant nine months in Le Gros Caillou *quartier* in the 7th arr., just a few hundred metres from the Parc du Champ de Mars and its gigantic metal edifice, the Eiffel Tower. It was at this address working in a 'dreary room in a dreary hotel' that Joyce began his second epic work, *Finnegans Wake*, revealing the title, some months later, only to Nora. According to his biographer, Gordon Bowker, Joyce had gone to Bognor in Sussex with his family that summer and whilst there had begun to put into order some 40 pages of notes left over from *Ulysses* and had then used this material to start his new work.

Restful holidays on the channel coasts of France and England, Etretat and Dieppe were favourites, or on the Riviera or in nearby Belgium, Switzerland and Germany were the way that Joyce often unwound especially when his eye problems became too overwhelming. However, it was not all dreariness at rue Blaise Desgoffe for the Joyces, as they had many happy evenings at the nearby Restaurant les Trianons where they dined almost daily and also wined and dined their friends and amazed the restaurant staff with the generosity of their tips.

After moving to a larger and brighter room in the Victoria Palace and after a fruitful sojourn in Brittany, James and Nora finally found a flat available for six months, again in Avenue Charles Floquet. The 7th arr. and particularly the quietly residential area around Ave Bosquet where they spent in all ten and a half years between Square de Robiac and rue Edmond Valentin, less than two thirds of a kilometre from each other, seems to have been their favourite area in Paris. Moving to Square de Robiac in May 1925 the Joyces finally came into their own with nine rooms at their disposal including three living rooms and a drawing room and a room for a live in Breton housemaid.

It was here in November 1927 that Joyce invited a select group of friends to listen to a reading of the now finished *Anna Livia Plurabelle* including Maria and Eugene Jolas, Mary and Padraic Colum, Hemingway and Larbaud, twenty five guests in all. David Pritchard in his biography of Joyce says *Finnegans Wake* of which *Anna Livia Plurabelle* was an extract was 'the disciplined creation of a master writer working carefully to his own interior plan and logic' and was 'the literary equivalent of the paintings of Salvador Dali, Miro and Braque or the music of George Arnheim, one of whose compositions was scored for seven grand pianos, saws, hammers and an aeroplane propeller.' Point made!

It was also in Square de Robiac about this time that he was visited by Thomas MacGreevy who in 1928 was to introduce Beckett to him and his old friend from Dublin, J F Byrne, who according to Gordon Bowker, delighted him by reading *Anna Livia Plurabelle* aloud in a pure Dublin accent. However, Joyce's brother,

Stanislaus, when he came to Square de Robiac was not impressed by any of this and was not afraid to tell him, 'You have done the longest day in literature, and now you are conjuring up the deepest night.' Further criticism of his *Work In Progress* particularly from Ezra Pound and his patron and principal supporter, Harriet Shaw Weaver, almost weakened Joyce's resolve to continue with his epic work but he finally decided that 'the night world cannot be represented in the language of the day' and courageously kept on course.

The eighteen or so months between April 1931 when the Joyces left Square de Robiac and finally moved into a new apartment in rue Galilee (8th arr.) in November 1932 were turbulent and unsettled for the family. During this period they were to stay mainly in hotels in the admittedly fashionable 8th arrondissement with two longer stays in flats they leased, one in Campden Grove in Kensington in London and one in Avenue St Philibert in Passy. Altogether they stayed in six different addresses in this period: Hotel Powers, rue Francois Premier, 28 Campden Grove, La Residence, Avenue Pierre Premier de Serbie, Avenue St Philibert, Hotel Belmont et de Bassano, rue de Bassano and Hotel Lord Byron, Champs Elysees. This was what no doubt occasioned Louis Gillet, an art historian and critic, who became a friend of Joyce in the thirties, to make his observation about Joyce not really having 'settled' in Paris. During this period too Giorgio married the previously married Helen Fleischmann much against the wishes of his mother and the marriage was the catalyst for the move to London and all the ensuing upheaval, the move being officially designated by Joyce as another 'hegira'. The move and ongoing drama also probably exacerbated Lucia's increasingly severe illness.

However, relative calm and stability returned late in 1932 when Joyce took out a lease on a small but expensive furnished flat in rue Galilee just off the Champs Elysees and a stone's throw from the Arc de Triomphe. This was to be their home until September 1934 when they would move to rue Edmond Valentin their second longest place of residence in Paris, a quiet and unremarkable street off Avenue Bosquet and not ten minutes walk from Square de Robiac, so the area was completely familiar. It was here that Joyce was finally to complete his *Work In Progress* in 1938, fulfilling the overwhelming task which according to Adrienne Monnier he had imposed on himself when he wrote *Ulysses* the elevation of 'the mysticism of the human... the invention and composition of an inventory of the sensible world.' The Joyces were to stay in rue Edmond Valentin for four and a half years moving briefly to rue des Vignes off Avenue Mozart in Passy and not far from their very first flat in Paris, in rue de l'Assomption, before moving in October 1939 to their final Paris address, fittingly perhaps, the Hotel Lutetia in Boulevard Raspail.

Joyce's years in Paris were cut short by the outbreak of war in the autumn of 1939. There had indeed been many moves there but usually for pressing reasons and the city itself was a refuge for Joyce offering him a security, acceptance and fulfilment that might not have been possible for him anywhere else. Jean Michel Rabate, writing in the Cambridge Companion to Joyce, says that Paris in 1920 was almost designed for someone like Joyce. Pound's invitation was spot on. Not only was Paris the place of intellectual ferment and post war release it was also the artistic and literary crossroads not just of Europe but of the world with an influx of young writers from America, attracted by the very favourable franc - dollar exchange rate and another influx of people young and old from Eastern Europe in the turmoil after the Revolution in Russia. Russian émigrés, writers, artists and composers flocked to Paris in ever increasing numbers after Trotsky's Red Army had successfully defended the Revolution against attempts to restore the status quo.

Paris was the place where creative people came from all over to perfect their skills, promote their ideas and their work and to gain further inspiration in the heady atmosphere of a city tolerant of avant garde experimentation and alive with intellectual conversation and debate. For Joyce, Paris was 'the last of the human cities', a cultural oasis, a place where he could feel secure and able to operate at a safe distance from enemies, real or imagined, where he could feel welcomed and among friends even though his heart would always be in Dublin. Rabate points out that Paris was the city which took to his Homeric epic with an enthusiasm not attained elsewhere until many year afterwards, and remarks on the interest in things Homeric already generated in Paris in 1920 by the publication of Anatole France's *Le Cyclope* and the putting on in the same year of Gabriel Faure's, *Penelope* at the Opera.

If Paris had offered Joyce the security and the favourable conditions to thrive, he in turn, enriched not only the city's cultural life by making it the centre of world literary attention with the publication there of his *chef d 'oeuvre, Ulysses* by Sylvia Beach's Shakespeare & Company and with the frequent readings of his mysterious *Work In Progress* but also its everyday life in his dealings with the city's waiters and restaurant staff, taxi drivers, concierges, lavatory attendants, dustmen and postmen all of whom benefited from his lavish generosity, it can be confidently said that Joyce did not hold on to his money. For Joyce also every life had a heroism of its own and as Declan Kiberd reminds us in *Ulysses and Us, The Art of Everyday Living,* an interest of its own. Joyce's epic work, despite its Homeric framework and classical foundation and immense but lightly worn erudition is in many ways a celebration of the ordinary man and woman, of the extraordinary richness of everyday life and of the wisdom and stoicism and frequent kindness of the people who do the mundane tasks that make so much else possible.

In June 1920 Joyce had written to his aunt in Dublin that he was bringing his family to England then Ireland and en route would stay in Paris for a week. However, after Trieste, Pola, Rome and Zurich and many tribulations he had arrived in just the right place, at just the right time. There was a lot of hard work and eye problems and drama ahead but things began to fall into place and really could not have been that much more perfect, Joyce *etait atterri enfin!*

SEINE ET LIFFEY

Schr...ill crying seagulls ecstatic.... hovering over Lutetia's
Or is it Eblana's flotsam and jetsom... Swoo...oop a gull
Alights on fast swelling fleuve with aquatic fluency
Eager plaintive cries punctuate city's humdrum and
Thrill Liffey lorn exile on the quay late morn.

Further along tap... tap... tap, M'Sieu, pour l'amour de Dieu,
Un sou pas plus.. softly persisting voice.. tap.. tap... tap as
Mutile de la guerre claims his share under darkening sky.
Splat! The first drop falls... splitter... splutter.. splat again

Splink! A coin...a franc! Then quickening drumbeat as cloud
Bursts and torrent merges exile, beggar, sky and river
Sending seagulls diving along the Seine schr...ill crying....

Seine et Liffey   Brian O'Shea copyright 2011.

SELECTED PASSAGES FROM FINNEGANS WAKE

*(Joyce takes an encyclopaedic, kaleidoscopic, seriously comic
look at life, relationships, mankind, religion, science, geography
and history through the prism of Dublin and environs...as Edna
O'Brien notes in her biography of Joyce: 'Edgar Quinet whom he
admired was paid the honour of having a piece of his prose
ceremoniously moved from Illyria and Numantia to the environs
of Dublin - "the cornflowers have been staying at Ballymun, the
duskrose has choosed out Goatstown's hedges, twolips have
pressed togatherthem by sweet Rush..." ')*

This is a passage on food and religion:

'O.K Oh Kosmos! Ah Ireland! A.I. And for kailkannonkabbis
gimme Cincinattis with Italian but *(ci vuol poco)* ciccalick cheese.
Haggis good, haggis strong, haggis never say die. For quid we
have recipimus, recipe, O lout! And save that, Oliveiro, for thy
sunny day! Soupmeagre! Couldn't look at it! But if you'll buy me
yon coat of the vairy furry best, I'll try and pull it awn mee. It's in
fairly good order and no doubt 'twill sarve to turn. Remove this
boardcloth! Next stage, tell the tabler, for a variety of Huguenot
ligooms i'll try my set on edges grapeling an aigrydoucks, grilled
over birchen rods, with a few bloomancowls in albies> I want to
get outside monasticism. Mass and meat mar no man's journey.
Eat a missal lest. Nuts for the nerves, a flitch for the flue and for
to rejoice the chambers of the heart the spirits of the spice isles,
curry and cinnamon, chutney and cloves. All the vitalmines is
beginning to sozzle in chewn and the hormonies to clingleclange,
fudgem, kates and eaps and naboc and erics and oinnos on
kingclud and xoxxoxo and xooxox xxoxoxxoxxx till I'm fustfed
like fungstif and very presently form now posthaste its off yourll
see me ryuoll and on my usual rounds again to draw Terminus
Lower and Killadown and Letternoosh, Letterspeak, Lettermuck
to Littorananima and the roomiest house even in Ireland, if you

can understamp that…..

A lyrical description of Issy, Isabelle, Isolde daughter of Anna Livia Plurabelle:

Night by silent sailing night while infantine Isobel (who will be blushing all day to be, when she growed up one Sunday, Saint Holy and Saint Ivory, when she took the veil, the beautiful presentation nun, so barely twenty, in her pure coif, sister Isobel, and next Sunday, Mistlemas, when she looked a peach, the beautiful Samaritan, still as beautiful and still in her teens, nurse Saintette Isabelle, with stiffstarched cuffs but on Holiday, Christmas, Easter mornings when she wore a wreath, the wonderful widow of eighteen springs, Madame Isa Veuve La Belle, so sad but lucksome in her boyblue's long black with orange blossoming weeper's veil for she was the only girl they loved, as she is the queenly pearl you prize, because of the way the night that first we met she is bound to be, methinks, and not in vain, the darling of my heart, sleeping in her april cot, within her singachamer, with her greengageflavoured candywhistleduetted to the crazy quilt, Isobel, she is so pretty, truth to tell, wildwood's eyes and primarose hair, quietly, all the woods so wild, in mauves of moss and daphnedews, how all so still she lay, neath of the whitethorn, child of tree, like some losthappy leaf, like blowing flower stilled, as fain would she anon, for soon again 'twill be, win me, woo me, wed me, ah weary me! deeply, now evencalm lay sleeping……

The coming of nightfall…

'It darkles (tinct, tint) all this our funnanimal world. Yon marshpond by ruodmark verge is visited by the tide. Alvemmarea! We are circumveiloped by obscuritads. Man and belves frieren. There is a wish on them to be not doing or anything. Or just for rugs. Zoo koud. Drr, deff, coal lay on and, pzz, call us pyrress!

Ha! Where is our highly honourworthy salutable spouse
founderess? The foolish one of the family is within. Haha.
Huzoor, where's he? At house, to's pitty. With Nancy Hands.
Tseetshee. Hound through the maize has fled. What hou! Isegrim
under lolling ears. Far wol! And wheaten bells bide breathless.
All. The trail of Gill is not yet to be seen, rocksdrops, up benn,
down dell, a craggy road for rambling. Nor yet through starland
that silver sash. What era's o'ering? Lang gone late. Say long,
scielo! Sillume, see lo! Selene, sail O! Amune! Ark!? Noh?!
Nought stirs in spinney. The swayful pathways of the dragonfly
spider stay still in reedery. Quiet takes back her folded fields.
Tranquille thanks. Adew. In deerhaven, imbraced, alleged,
injoynted and unlatched, the birds tommelise too, quail silent.'

Dawn....

Eftsoon so too will our sphoenix spark spirt his spyre and sunward
stride the rampante flambe. Ay, already the sombrer opacities of
the gloom are sphanished! Brave footsore Haun! Work your
progress! Hold to! Now! Win out, ye divil ye! The silent cock
shall crow at last. The west shall shake the east awake. Walk while
ye have the night for morn, lightbreakfastbringer, morroweth
whereon every past shall full fost sleep. Amain.

BECKETTS REFLECTIONS on SAINT LÔ
An excerpt from The World of Samuel Beckett: 1906-1946 by Lois Gordon.

After Beckett returned to Paris - the time of his great creative "siege" - he wrote the radio speech "The Capital of the Ruins" (June 10, 1946). The speech was occasioned by Dublin press coverage of France's ostensible lack of appreciation of the Irish effort in Saint-Lô. Beckett's intention was reconciliatory, to praise both the French and the Irish. However, his decision to make a public statement - exceptional for this man - and the nature of that statement deserve close inspection, for Beckett is atypically explicit in his philosophical reflections. We know, in retrospect, that the end of the war marked a major turning point in his life; in this speech, Beckett went beyond the Saint-Lô experience to express a vision derived from his entire life thus far. He would later say that he wrote from "impotence" and "ignorance", but there is a sense here of his own wisdom and self confidence. Perhaps for just this moment Beckett experienced a sense of "knowing" and a conviction of his own courage. Perhaps these were to be the foundation for his retreat to "the room," during which he engaged the world of his imagination. Beckett was forty when he wrote the speech.

In this beautiful and moving statement, Beckett exalts both the comfort to be drawn from the inward human capacity to surmount circumstances of the utmost gravity and the sustenance to be given and gained in moments of camaraderie. He also sets forth several articles of faith which will resonate throughout his great works to come.

The first is his awareness of the human capacity to endure the caprices of circumstance: "What was important was not our having penicillin… [but] the occasional glimpse obtained, by us in them [the patients] and, who knows, by them in us… of that smile at the human condition as little to be extinguished by bombs as to

be broadened by the elixirs of Burroughes and Welcome, the smile
deriding, among other things, the having and not having, the
giving and the taking, sickness and health." The "smile deriding…
the having and not having" would become, in *Waiting for Godot*,
that which enables humanity to face the fact that "The tears of the
world are a constant quantity." The smile also enables the
consolation one derives from the corollary truth that "the same is
true of the laugh."

Beckett's second point would seem to be that while the material
universe is "provisional" and ephemeral, acts of mundane
generosity are not: "The hospital of wooden huts and its gardens
between the Vire and Bayeux roads will continue to discharge its
function, and its cured. 'Provisional' is not the term it was in this
universe become provisional. It will continue to discharge its
function long after the Irish are gone." Beckett would seem to be
extolling the human impulse to give of oneself to the suffering. It
is this that is a steadfast thread in the human fabric, an aspect of
life that is not provisional. Implicit in this remark is Beckett's
contrast between the abiding nature of the human spirit and the
transitory trappings of worldly power, between the permanence of
generosity and the impermanent edifices of the material world.
Also implicit here is his faith, as he again writes in *Waiting for
Godot*, that regardless of circumstance, humanity will "represent
worthily the foul brood to which a cruel fate has consigned us."

In perhaps his most optimistic statement, Beckett declares that the
act of giving uplifts the giver as well as the recipient: "Those who
were in Saint-Lô will come home realising that they got at least as
good as they gave." This may be our salvation as we await Godot.

Beckett would proceed to evoke artistically increasingly sparse
human habitations, and his worlds and its figures would seem to
pale in comparison with, say, James Joyce's grand invocations of
human possibility. But Beckett, perhaps more so than Joyce, had

come to understand the limitations imposed upon the individual by powerful and eternally unpredictable inner and outer forces - the limits posed by the absurdity of the human condition. In this remarkable radio speech, Beckett defines what we come to intuit in his later work as life's redeeming virtues. The individual's fate may be provisional, and the course of history may be provisional, but the "smile" that derides the conditional is not. Its source is in the human spirit, and from this comes healers of a moment - those who build hospitals, those who dance a jig, and those who would entertain a reader. The hospitals, like the dancers and the names of fictional characters, will fade, just as the names of the ordinary Irish or French patriots will be forgotten - but the spirit that moves them will not.

Finally, as a man of specific place and origin - always rooted in this world and certainly not an artist-would-be-god or an unworldly aesthete - Beckett stresses that the *Irish* in Saint-Lô demonstrated the best part of human nature, that quality that seeks to heal or console, rather than to dominate or desolate. With evident Irish pride he adds: "I think that to the end of its hospital days, it will be called the Irish Hospital, and after that the huts, when they have been turned into dwellings, the Irish huts."

At the end of the speech, revealing what was perhaps for him the most crucial wisdom that would direct his future work, he adds: "I may perhaps venture to mention another [possibility], more remote but perhaps of greater import... the possibility that [*those in Saint-Lô*]... *got indeed what they could hardly give, a vision and a sense of time-honoured concept of humanity in ruins, and perhaps even an inkling of the terms in which our condition is to be thought again*. These will have been in France" (emphasis added). The willingness to give of oneself to the suffering is not only an abiding part of human nature. It is also the very means through which one can gain an "inkling" of the mystery of the human condition.

When Beckett wrote this speech, he had already resigned his post at Saint-Lô and was settled in Paris. This speech was thus one of his earliest postwar writings. Indeed, his earlier remark about the endurance of the Irish spirit and his final reminder that these lessons will have been consummated in France reconcile the land of his origin with the land of his destiny.

In addressing "our condition"… to be thought again" Beckett braces himself for the great creative task now facing him.

Beckett was not a fragile and reclusive man set apart from the real world. He was a sensitive and courageous man, marked by and responsive to the world around him. Every city he lived in, every friend he made, every painting he studied, and every writer he read - all became a part of the man and part of his art. Brother fighting and consoling brother, the individual seeking meaning and sustenance from within and without, the capacity for humour which enables the spirit to transcend the harm that human nature and the human condition impose - those would be "thought again" in the works to come.

JOYCE AND BECKETT SOCIETIES AND CENTRES

Joyce Societies and Centres
The epicentre of all things Joycean must surely be the James Joyce Centre in Dublin. Their address is:

35 North Great George's Street Dublin 1. tel. 00 353 1 878 8547.
Email: info@jamesjoyce.ie

But needless to say there are James Joyce societies around the world, from the American Friends of James Joyce to the Zurich James Joyce Foundation, some of which are in the following list:

American Friends of James Joyce
James Joyce Society of Bahia Blanca
James Joyce Society of Copenhagen (and of Denmark)
Finnegans Wake Society of New York
Hungarian James Joyce Society
Iberjoyce
International James Joyce Foundation
James Joyce Italian Foundation
James Joyce Society of Japan
James Joyce Society of Korea
James Joyce Society (New York) Rosenbach Museum and Library
Sarasota James Joyce Society
South Side James Joyce Society
James Joyce Society of Sweden and Finland
Syracuse James Joyce Club
Trieste Joyce Summer School
UCD James Joyce Research Centre
Zurich James Joyce Foundation

We have probably missed many others but just write in and let us know and your society will be added on. And of course, there are all the reading groups unfortunately space does not permit...

JOYCE AND BECKETT SOCIETIES AND CENTRES

Beckett Societies and Centres
The Samuel Beckett Society - University of Antwerp
American Samuel Beckett Society
Dutch Samuel Beckett Society
Gare St Lazare Players
The Godot Company
Samuel Beckett Gesellschaft, International Samuel Beckett Society
Samuel Beckett Society of Israel
Samuel Beckett Research Circle of Japan
La Maison Samuel Beckett
The Samuel Beckett Centre TCD
The Samuel Beckett International Foundation (University of Reading).

SOME JOURNALS and WEBSITES
Buffalo Bloomsday Exhibition
International James Joyce Foundation
James Joyce Journal
James Joyce Literary Supplement
James Joyce and Music
James Joyce Quarterly
James Joyce Webring
Joyce Images
Joyce Studies Annual
Joycean Japan
www.joycesociety.org
www.modernword.com/joyce (The Brazen Head)
Journal of Beckett Studies
Samuel Beckett Today/Aujourd'hui
Samuel Beckett Endpage
(official page of The Samuel Beckett Society - a multiple resource site
for all those interested in Beckett's life and works)
Le Cercle de Beckett
Apmonia - www.modernword.com/beckett
The Thomas MacGreevy Archive

BIBLIOGRAPHY

Beckett
A. Alvarez   Woburn   1973

James Joyce
Chester G. Anderson   Thames & Hudson   1967

The Joyce We Knew: Cambridge Companion To James Joyce
Derek Attridge   Cambridge University Press   2004

Beckett L'Increvable Desir
Alain Badiou   Hachette Litteratures   2007

Samuel Beckett: A Biography
Deirdre Bair   Harvest / HBJ   1980

The Genius of the Irish Theater
Ed. Sylvan Barnett, Morton Berman and William Burton
                                  New American Library   1960

The Bloomsday Book
Harry Blamires   Methuen   1966

A Preface To James Joyce
Sydney Bolt   Longman   1992

James Joyce: A New Biography
Gordon Bowker   MacMillan   2012

James Joyce And The Making of Ulysses
Frank Budgen   Indiana University Press   1960

Samuel Becket: The Last Modernist
A.J Cronin   Flamingo   1997

Hemingway: The Grace and The Pressure
Aubrey Dillon Malone   Robson   1999

Selected Letters of James Joyce
R. Ellmann   Faber & Faber   1975

Paris City Guide
Steve Fallon and Annabel Hart Lonely Planet   2006

About Beckett: The Playwright & The Work
John Fletcher   Faber and Faber   2003

Man's Search For Meaning
Viktor Frankl   Touchstone Press   1959

The World of Samuel Beckett: 1906 - 1946
Lois Gordon   Yale University Press   1996

Expatriate Paris:
A Cultural and Literary Guide to the Paris of the 1920s
A.J. Hansen   Arcade   1990

A Moveable Feast
Ernest Hemingway   Arrow Books   2011

Seven Ages of Paris - Portrait of a City
Alistair Home   MacMillan   2002

Ulysses OUP edition
Jeri Johnson   Oxford University Press   1998

The Irish Mind - Exploring Intellectual Traditions
Richard Kearney (Ed.)   Wolfhound   1985

Ulysses and Us, The Art of Everyday Living
Declan Kiberd   Faber and Faber   2009

Damned To Fame: The Life of Samuel Beckett
James Knowlson   Bloomsbury   1996

Paris: A Literary Companion
I. Littlewood   Murray   1987

Finding Godot
Declan McCavana   The Irish Eyes   October 2004

Joyce for Beginners
David Norris & Carl Flint   Flint Icon Books   1994

James Joyce
Edna O'Brien   Penguin   1999

Brendan Behan
Ulick O'Connor   Hamish Hamilton   1970

Memoirs of Joyce
Ulick O'Connor (ed.)   Brandon   2004

Samuel Beckett
J. Pilling   Routledge & Kegan Paul   1976

James Joyce
David Pritchard   Geddes & Grosset   2001

Fermat's Last Theorem
Simon Singh   Fourth Estate Limited   1997

Samuel Beckett: Six Residua   Calder Publications   1999

Samuel Beckett: Three Novellas   Calder Publications   1999

Tourist Guide – Paris   Michelin et Cie Proprietaires 1981

Plan de Paris   Michelin   1981-2

Paris du Nord au Sud   Michelin   2007

READERS NOTES

READERS NOTES